AMERICANS 1942

18 ARTISTS FROM 9 STATES

AMERICANS

THE MUSEU

1942

18 ARTISTS FROM 9 STATES

EDITED BY DOROTHY C. MILLER

WITH STATEMENTS BY THE ARTISTS

F MODERN ART, NEW YORK

PRINTED IN THE UNITED STATES OF AMERICA

CONTENTS

Acknowledgments

On behalf of the President and Trustees of the Museum of Modern Art I wish to thank the artists in the exhibition for their contributions to the catalog and for their assistance in assembling their work for the exhibition; and the collectors, institutions and dealers who have lent to the exhibition. In addition, I am grateful for the generous assistance of the following: Jere Abbott; Fred Bartlett; Donald J. Bear; Fred Biesel; Clyde H. Burroughs; Jerry Bywaters; Holger Cahill; Kenneth Callahan; Thaddeus Clapp; Val Clear; Mrs. Walter Davenport; Robert Tyler Davis; Dr. G. H. Edgell; Lorser Feitelson; Edward W. Forbes; Mrs. Juliana R. Force; Dr. Walter R. Hepner; Mrs. Lydia Herrick Hodge; Mrs. Mildred Holzhauer; Richard Hood; Richard Foster Howard; R. Bruce Inverarity; Roland J. McKinney; Dr. Grace L. McCann Morley; Richard C. Morrison; John O'Connor, Jr.; Lloyd J. Reynolds; Daniel Catton Rich; Robert A. Rosenbaum; Edward B. Rowan; Mrs. Alice M. Sharkey; Frederick Shipman; Mrs. Margery Hoffman Smith; Miss Frances Strain; Mark Tobey; Dr. W. R. Valentiner; S. Macdonald-Wright. The WPA Art Program has allowed the use of statements by Hord, Levine and Siporin which were prepared for the Program.

Dorothy C. Miller
Director of the Exhibition

Lenders to the Exhibition

Mr. and Mrs. Lee A. Ault, New Canaan, Conn.; Mr. and Mrs. Donald J. Bear, Santa Barbara, Cal.; Hon. and Mrs. Robert Woods Bliss, Santa Barbara, Cal.; Hyman Bloom, Boston; Samuel Cashwan, Detroit; Mrs. Morris Cafritz, Washington, D. C.; Francis Chapin, Chicago; Mr. and Mrs. Hugh Chisholm, Beverly Hills, Cal.; Mrs. Henry L. Corbett, Portland, Ore.; Mrs. Walter Davenport, Winsted, Conn.; Miss Emma Lu Davis, Los Angeles; Mrs. H. L. Edwards, Dallas; Mr. and Mrs. Hollis Farwell, Seattle; Lee Foley, Seattle; Dr. and Mrs. Lindel French, San Francisco; Dr. Richard E. Fuller, Seattle; Mrs. Jan de Graaff, Portland, Ore.; Morris Graves, Seattle; Charles Howard, San Francisco; Mrs. John Galen Howard, Berkeley, Cal.; Mrs. Marquis James, Pleasantville, N. Y.; Arthur Judson, New York; Dr. A. Gurney Kimberley, Portland, Ore.; Mr. and Mrs. Benjamin Laskin, Germantown, Pa.; Rico Lebrun, Santa Barbara, Cal.; Jack Levine, Boston; Mr. and Mrs. Samuel A. Lewisohn, New York; Jesse Lilienthal, Hillsborough, Cal.; Wright Ludington, Santa Barbara, Cal.; Miss Helen Lundeberg, Los Angeles; Edwin J. Lukas, White Plains, N. Y; Miss Aline MacMahon, New York; Dr. and Mrs. Leslie M. Maitland, West Los Angeles; Octavio Medellin, Denton, Tex.; Knud Merrild, Los Angeles; George Palmer, Boston; Mr. and Mrs. Channing Peake, Santa Barbara, Cal.; Mrs. James S. Plaut, Cambridge, Mass.; Charles Pollock, Detroit; David L. Podell, New York; Miss Margaret Prall, Berkeley, Cal.; George P. Raymond, New York; Miss Helen Resor, Mrs. Stanley Resor, and Stanley Rogers Resor, Greenwich, Conn.; Mr. and Mrs. Frank Rosengren, San Antonio, Tex.; Mr. and Mrs. Charles Ross, Seattle; Edward B. Rowan, Falls Church, Va.; Mr. and Mrs. Joseph T. Ryerson, Chicago; Mr. and Mrs. Arthur Sachs, Santa Barbara, Cal.; Mr. and Mrs. Max Schott, New York, Nat Sharfman, Boston; Herman Shulman, New York; Mr. and Mrs. Samuel Spewack, New Hope, Pa.; Everett Spruce, Austin, Tex.; Vladimir Golschmann, St. Louis; Mrs. J. Rosenbaum, Bloomfield, Conn.

Associated American Artists, New York; Boyer Galleries, New York; Downtown Gallery, New York; Dalzell Hatfield Galleries, Los Angeles; Midtown Galleries, New York; Oregon Ceramic Studio, Portland; Perls Galleries, New York; Weyhe Gallery, New York.

Museum of Fine Arts, Boston; Fogg Museum of Art, Harvard University, Cambridge; Art Institute of Chicago; Dallas Museum of Fine Arts; Southern Methodist University, Dallas; Detroit Institute of Arts; Franklin D. Roosevelt Library, Hyde Park; Los Angeles County Museum; Whitney Museum of American Art, New York; Smith College Museum of Art, Northampton, Mass.; Reed College, Portland, Ore.; San Diego State College; San Francisco Museum of Art; Santa Barbara Museum of Art; Work Projects Administration Art Program.

Trustees of the Museum

HONORARY TRUSTEES

Staff of the Museum

FOREWORD

Americans 1942 is the first of a series of exhibitions which the Museum of Modern Art is planning and which will provide a continuing survey of the arts in the United States during the 1940's. The first exhibition of the series, *18 Artists from 9 States*, is a selection limited by definition and by necessity to a small number of painters and sculptors whose work is new to the New York public or has not been adequately represented here in recent years. Artists closely identified with the New York art world have not been included in this year's exhibition, but succeeding shows in the series will not be limited in this way.

The number of artists in the exhibition has been kept small in order that each might be represented by a group of works sufficient to give an indication of style and personality. New York artists and the New York public will make the acquaintance in this show of at least two painters whose names and pictures are unknown to them. Several others, though not complete strangers, have never had a one-man exhibition in New York. Of the rest, some are newcomers who have made their mark in the last year or two, others have been showing for some years but have never been well known in the east.

Most of them have studied and worked in towns far removed from the art centers of the Atlantic seaboard—some, in fact, have never been in the east. They come from Texas, California, Oregon, Washington, Missouri, Michigan, Illinois, Pennsylvania, Massachusetts—and these are only a few of the states where one may discover high talent and sound training in the arts.

Americans 1942 underscores the remarkable development of important art centers throughout the country in the past decade. The United States Government art programs have had much to do with this development. With few exceptions the artists in this exhibition have been sponsored, at one time or another, by the Section of Fine Arts of the Public Buildings Administration or by the WPA Art Program.

Younger artists predominate and their recent work has been favored. Five of the men are past forty but the average age of the eighteen artists is thirty-five. The average date of the works in the exhibition is 1939. Succeeding shows of the series will follow the development not only of the younger artists but also that of our older and better known painters and sculptors who must not be lost sight of in our enthusiasm for new discoveries and youthful promise.

Americans 1942 covers a wide geographical range but the range of the work itself is even wider. Omnibus terms such as American scene, social comment, neo-romanticism, surrealism, and abstraction might be used to describe it, but much of it cannot be fitted into these categories. Some of the artists in the exhibition react in a highly personal way to an environment which has been closely observed and keenly felt. Others have a complex and cultivated approach to the artist's problem of mastery in his two worlds—the inner world of emotion and idea and the outer world of fact. Still others express a spiritual wrestling, an intense inner striving for a primary utterance of form.

All this is possible only in the liberty which our democracy gives to the artist. No regimentations, no compulsions or restrictions could call forth such richly various expressions of a people's creative spirit.

DOROTHY C. MILLER

The text of this book has been contributed largely by the artists, whose varying personalities and points of view are revealed in their brief statements. It may seem that the artists are represented somewhat unevenly, in the exhibition and in the book, in the number of their works shown. This is inevitable: sculptors in hard stone do not produce as much as watercolorists. In the case of certain painters whose pictures depend largely upon color and are unrewarding when reproduced in black and white, only a few have been illustrated.

DARREL AUSTIN

I'm afraid that those who read the following expecting to find the why and wherefore of my paintings will be disappointed. Had I something to say with words I would write a book. Some express themselves in verse or prose, others in music. I paint.

While painting I am never concerned with what the picture will look like to others. I cannot explain my paintings, they must be felt. However, there are certain technical details that can be described. For instance, I paint with a palette knife exclusively. I do not make preparatory sketches for my canvases, and I do not make direct use of a model.

I size my canvas and then apply the paint, usually with no preconceived idea of subject matter. When the final form emerges, the completion of the painting takes only a comparatively short while.

I have never been much interested in what other painters have done before me or are doing now.

DARREL AUSTIN

DARREL AUSTIN. The Black Beast. 1941. Oil on canvas, 24 x 30″. Lent by the Smith College Museum of Art, Northampton, Mass.

Darrel Austin was born in Raymond, Washington in 1907 and two years later moved to Portland, Oregon, where he grew up. He studied art at Columbia University, at Notre Dame and in Portland. The Belgian painter Emile Jacques was his favorite teacher although he disliked his painting.

In 1933 Austin began to paint on his own. A few years later, under the WPA Federal Art Project, he painted murals for the Medical College of the University of Oregon at Eugene. In 1938 he made a trip to southern California and had his first one-man show at the Putzel Gallery in Los Angeles. A second one-man show was held at the Perls Galleries, New York in 1940. He is represented in the collections of the Boston Museum of Fine Arts, the Albright Art Gallery, Buffalo, the Detroit Institute of Arts, the Metropolitan Museum of Art and the Museum of Modern Art, New York, and the Smith College Museum of Art, Northampton.

DARREL AUSTIN. The Legend. 1941. Oil on canvas, 30 x 24". Lent by the Perls Galleries, New York.

DARREL AUSTIN. Europa and the Bull. 1940. Oil on canvas, 30 x 36″. Lent by the Detroit Institute of Arts.

DARREL AUSTIN. The Vixen. 1941. Oil on canvas, 24 x 20″. Lent by the Museum of Fine Arts, Boston.

DARREL AUSTIN. Catamount. 1940. Oil on canvas, 20 x 24″. The Museum of Modern Art, Mrs. John D. Rockefeller, Jr. Purchase Fund.

Darrel Austin. Girl in the Brook. 1941. Oil on canvas, 20 x 15″. Lent by Miss Helen Resor, Greenwich, Conn.

HYMAN BLOOM

Hyman Bloom was born in Latvia on April 11, 1913. He came to America in 1920, landing in Boston. He has lived in Boston ever since.

For a time Bloom worked on the WPA Art Program, which owns several of his paintings. He has never had a one-man exhibition nor has his work been shown in New York before.

HYMAN BLOOM. The Synagogue (detail, first version). *c.* 1940. Oil on canvas, 65¼ x 46¼″. Lent by the artist.

HYMAN BLOOM. The Synagogue (second version). *c.* 1940. Oil on canvas, 39 x 30⅛″. Lent by the Massachusetts WPA Art Program.

HYMAN BLOOM. Skeleton. *c.* 1936. Oil on canvas, 12 x 68″. Lent by Nat Sharfman, Boston.

Hyman Bloom. Jew with the Torah. *c.* 1940. Oil on canvas, 33 x 25″. Lent by the artist.

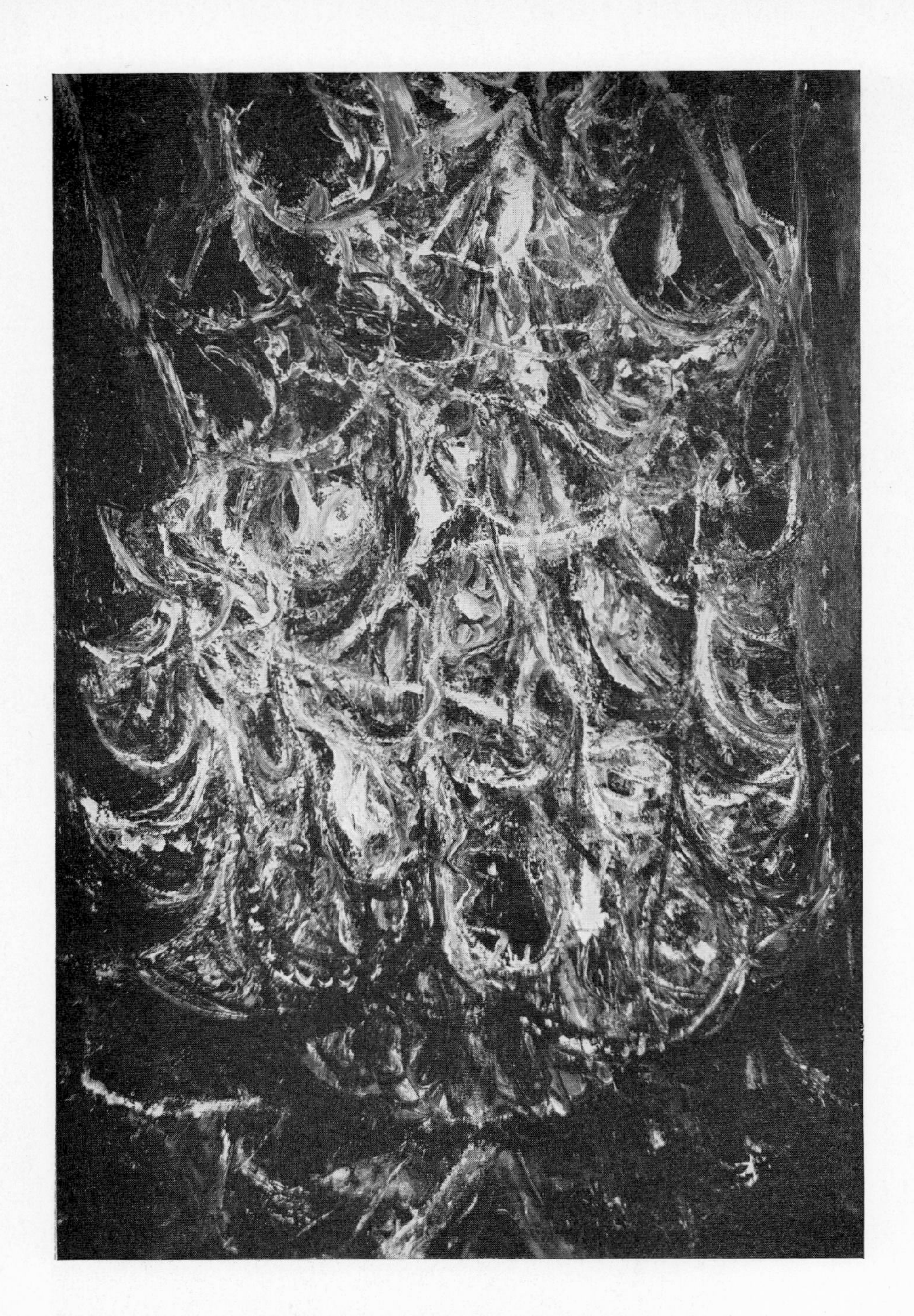

HYMAN BLOOM. The Christmas Tree. *c.* 1939. Oil on canvas, 54 x 35″. Lent by the artist.

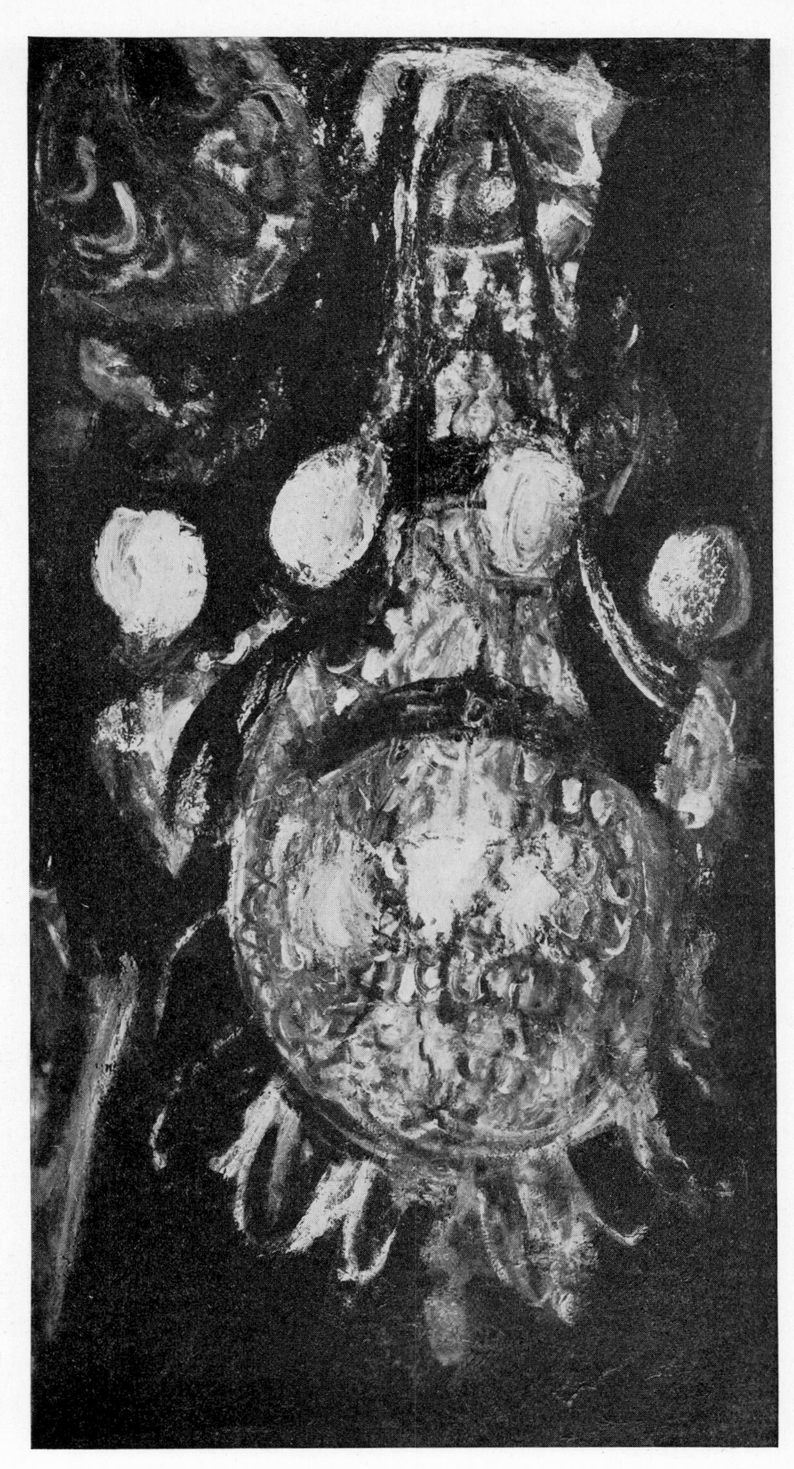

HYMAN BLOOM. The Chandelier. *c.* 1940. Oil on canvas, 72 x 36″. Lent by the artist.

RAYMOND BREININ

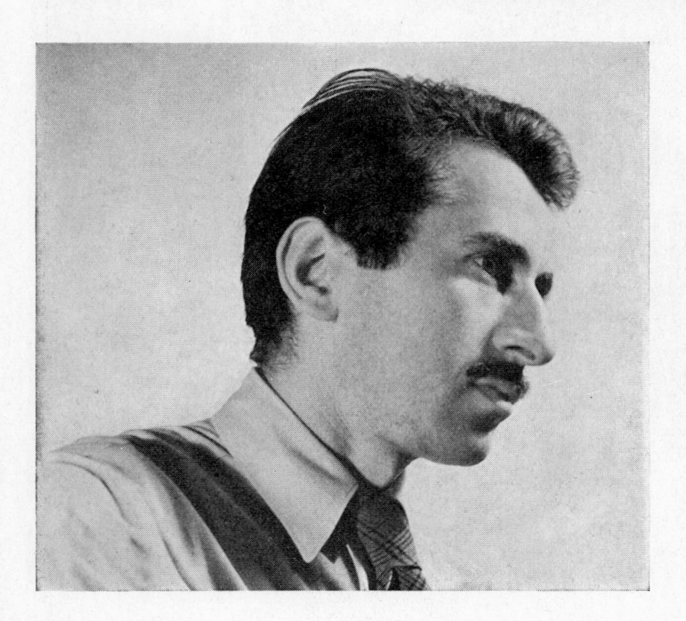

I was born in Vitebsk, Russia in 1909. My father's stories of pictures he had seen at the Hermitage and the Tretyakov Gallery in St. Petersburg must have had something to do with my early enrollment at the studio of the painter Uri Penn and, later, at the Vitebsk Academy of Art.

As I look back on those early days I spent in that ancient Russian city poised on the river Dvina, I feel that the atmosphere of that place and time still persists in my present-day thoughts. I recall the white cupola-topped Russian churches towering in their Byzantine majesty over a city of white houses; the market place, always colorful with peasant wares; the band in the park playing waltzes to its evening promenaders; visiting gypsies; the war—revolution—and changing regimes; and a long trip to America.

Here we arrived, a family of six, at Rochelle, Illinois, to remain for one year until we came to Chicago. After a short public school attendance, interrupted by lack of family prosperity, I found myself working successively at various jobs including commercial lithography, theatre poster painting, and running a hotel elevator. Whenever finances permitted I continued my art study, attending Saturday classes at the Art

Raymond Breinin. At Golgotha. 1941. Oil on canvas, 30 x 48″. Lent by the Downtown Gallery, New York.

Institute of Chicago and evenings at the Chicago Academy of Art. Between jobs I spent much of my time at the museum, altering my taste as time went on, from confusion, to French impressionism, to Cézanne, and finally to what I now regard as a less biased outlook.

Until recently, I was employed on the WPA Art Program, during which period I was able to devote all my time to painting.

Raymond Breinin

Commissioned by the Section of Fine Arts of the Public Buildings Administration Breinin painted a mural for the Post Office at Wilmette, Illinois. He had a one-man exhibition in New York at the Downtown Gallery in 1939. He is represented in the collections of the Fogg Museum of Art, Cambridge, the Brooklyn Museum, the Metropolitan Museum of Art and the Museum of Modern Art in New York, the San Francisco Museum of Art and the Zanesville (Ohio) Art Institute.

RAYMOND BREININ. Interior with Ancestor. 1939. Gouache, 16½ x 28″. Lent by the Downtown Gallery, New York.

RAYMOND BREININ. One Morning. 1939. Gouache, 16⅝ x 27⅝″. The Museum of Modern Art, Mrs. John D. Rockefeller, Jr. Purchase Fund.

RAYMOND BREININ. White House. 1938. Oil on canvas, 30 x 40⅛″. Lent by the WPA Art Program, Washington, D. C.

Raymond Breinin. The Lover's Return. 1941. Oil on canvas, 30 x 40″. Lent by the Downtown Gallery, New York.

RAYMOND BREININ. The Night. 1941. Gouache, 22 x 30″. Lent by the Downtown Gallery, New York.

SAMUEL CASHWAN

My background has been all good sculpture, with special leanings towards Romanesque and, later in life, Hindu. The remarkable craftsmanship, the crispness of style, and above all the sense of humor in Romanesque appealed to me then and does still. Hindu sculpture gave me a sense of the sobriety, the solidity, the eternity of form such as exists in organic growth. I am perhaps too close to my own work to realize to what extent these influences exist. If they do exist, I feel it is for the best.

I have been fortunate for many years in deriving a small income from teaching sculpture. This has allowed me some time to work creatively without the need to pot-boil or pander. I had need to experiment to find things out for myself, for above all I had no desire to adopt another's formula blindly. Sculpture like any other art is molded by social environment and tempered by the personality of the artist. There can, therefore, be no outright adoption of these laurel-bedecked formulas, many of which are already dead wood. In all my efforts I have tried to avoid adding to the useless heap of the "World's Fair" variety, the sensational, or the "just to be different."

I hold out for the near future when sculpture will find its true place. When it will be designedly integrated in dwellings and public buildings. When it will cease to be a showpiece or a collector's item and become a vital and essential part of a unified design for living.

SAMUEL CASHWAN

Samuel Cashwan was born in 1900 in Cherkassi near Kiev, Russia. He came to New York when he was a boy, later moving to Detroit where he still lives.

He studied at the Architectural League in New York and with Bourdelle in Paris. Returning to Detroit in 1927, he undertook several commissions, among them the façade sculpture and altar figure for St. Aloysius Church, and became instructor in architectural sculpture at the University of Michigan. At present he heads the sculpture department of the Detroit Society of Arts and Crafts.

Cashwan has completed many private sculpture commissions and since 1935 has done important architectural sculpture, as well as smaller work, for the WPA Art Program, for which he serves as sculpture supervisor in Michigan. Among his monumental works are reliefs for the Albion Band Shell, Detroit, for the Music Building, Michigan State College, Lansing, and for the municipal water conditioning plant, Lansing; and a head of Mark Twain for the Michigan State Normal School. He is represented in the collection of the Detroit Institute of Arts. He has never had a one-man exhibition of his work.

Front view of Torso illustrated on opposite page.

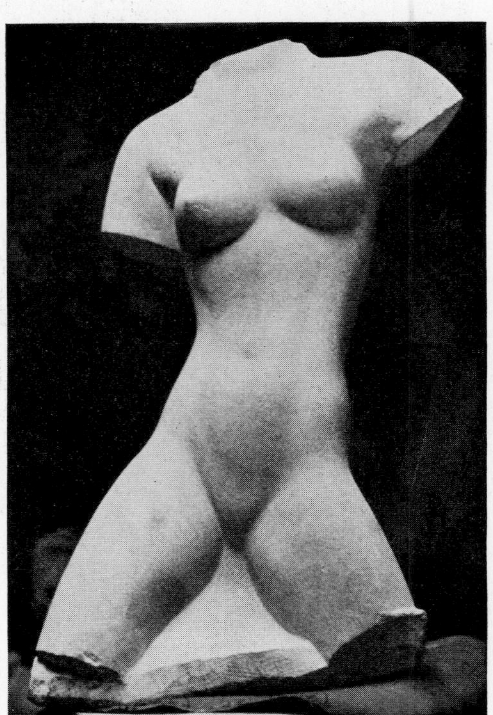

Samuel Cashwan. Torso. 1937. Limestone, 22″ high. Lent by the artist.

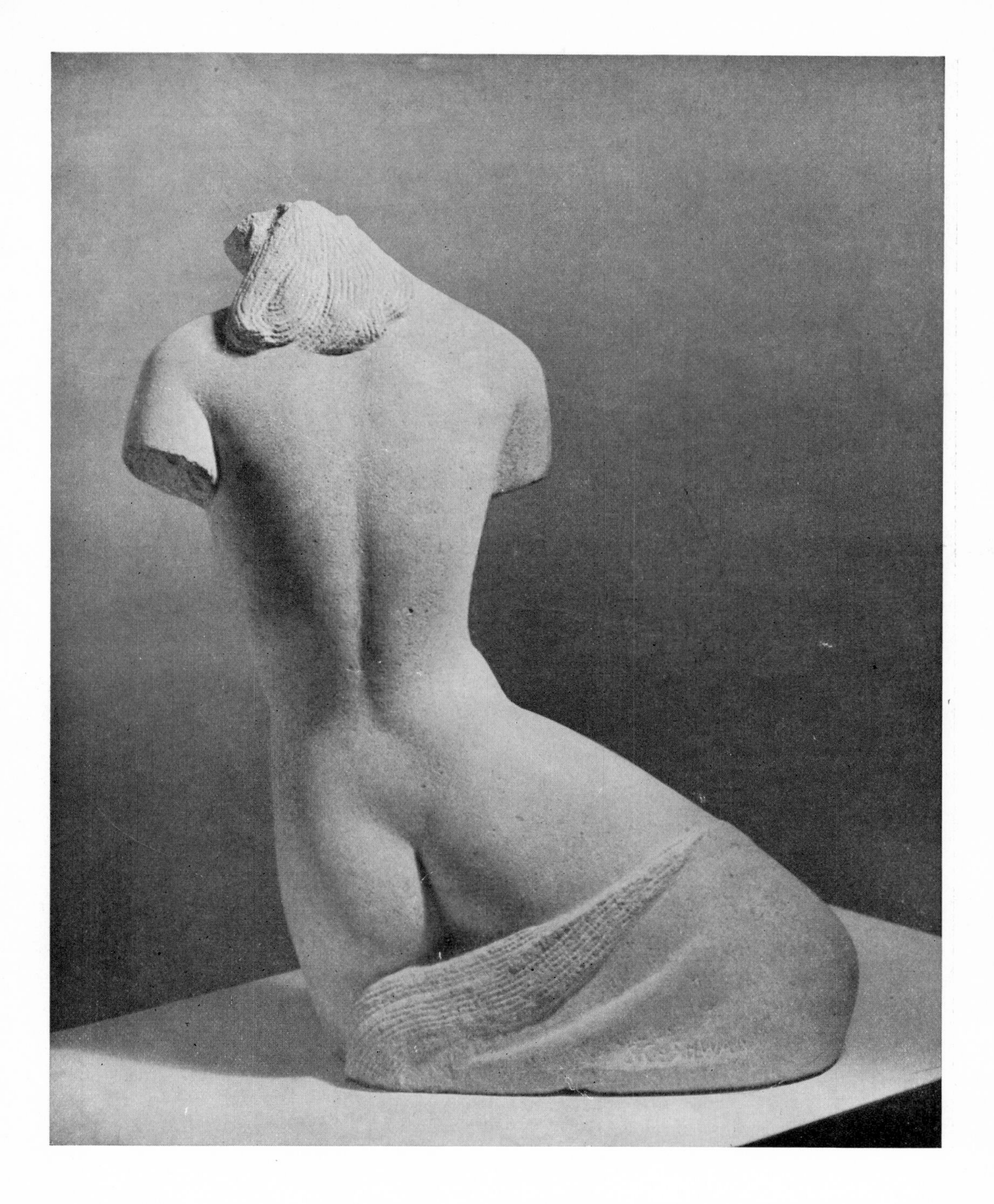

SAMUEL CASHWAN. Torso. 1936. Limestone, 23¾″ high. Lent by the WPA Art Program, Washington, D. C.

SAMUEL CASHWAN. Rising Figure. 1939. Mankato stone, 19½″ high. Lent by the Michigan WPA Art Program.

SAMUEL CASHWAN. Bather. 1937. Green marble, 14″ high. Lent by the artist.

SAMUEL CASHWAN. Baptism. 1938. Terra cotta, 7⅛″ high. Lent by the artist.

SAMUEL CASHWAN. The Prophet. 1937. Terra cotta, 9½″ high. Lent by the artist.

SAMUEL CASHWAN. Shelter. 1940. Terra cotta, 9″ high. Lent by the artist.

SAMUEL CASHWAN. Kneeling Torso. 1938. Terra cotta, 12″ high. Lent by the artist.

SAMUEL CASHWAN. Seated Figure. 1939. Terra cotta, 7½″ high. Lent by the artist.

FRANCIS CHAPIN

I duck when asked to explain painting or any particular one. I have always envied a remark by Malvin Albright, who when asked by a busy art critic and writer, "Just what are you trying to do in your sculpture?" answered, "Nothing." I like, too, the imposing article about a contemporary French painter which begins with a little self-appraisal by the artist: "I like sausage and fried potatoes."

Like everyone else who paints, I suppose, I would like my works to be truthful and to stay within the limits of their media—an oil painting being an oil, and a watercolor having painting truth applicable to a watercolor, and prints being in one color. Most murals and colored (indirect) prints seem to me to fall outside this "truthful" class—an entirely personal and possibly a temporary belief—because I seem to be moved mostly by the rightness of direct tonal and color values.

I haven't yet found a formula either for starting or carrying on a painting. There are many stimulating approaches that seem to be good to create an atmosphere of intensity of production, and I find them useful for myself as well as for others with whom I work.

Francis Chapin

FRANCIS CHAPIN. Children at Breakfast. 1939. Oil on canvas, 28 x 40″. Lent by the artist.

Francis Chapin was born in 1899 in Bristolville, Ohio. He finished high school there and was graduated in 1921 from Washington and Jefferson College. A year later he went to Chicago to the School of the Art Institute where he studied from 1922 to 1928. Next, the Bryan Lathrop Fellowship sent him to Europe where he spent a year painting, mostly in France. On his return to Chicago he had a one-man show at the Art Institute and another in the galleries of Carson, Pirie, Scott and Co. His one-man shows in New York, at the Ferargil Galleries in 1932 and the Macbeth Gallery in 1939 and 1940, have included only watercolors.

Chapin has been teaching lithography and painting at the School of the Art Institute of Chicago since 1930. He is represented in the collections of the Addison Gallery of American Art, Andover, the Brooklyn Museum, the Art Institute of Chicago and the Pennsylvania Academy of the Fine Arts, Philadelphia.

FRANCIS CHAPIN. Nude. 1941. Watercolor, 17½ x 12″. Lent by the artist.

FRANCIS CHAPIN. Spring Sunlight. 1938. Oil on canvas, 29 x 36″. Lent by the artist.

FRANCIS CHAPIN. Rutland Station. 1940. Watercolor, 21½ x 14¾″. Lent by the artist.

EMMA LU DAVIS

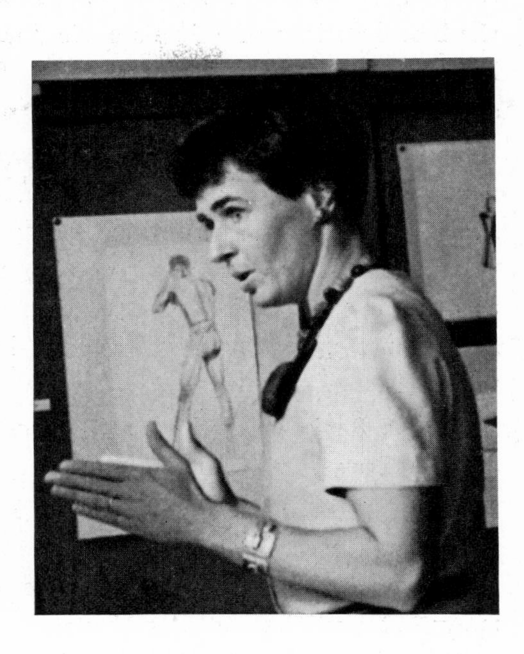

I was born in Indianapolis, Indiana, in November 1905, and continued to maintain a pretty high level of respectability until I came of age.

I was variously educated in Asbury Park public school, learning how to eat licorice sticks behind the third grade geography, and use, though not understand, bad words.

Long before the third grade, however, I drew and modeled, loving animals particularly. I suppose this was because even at the age of four or five I was endlessly fascinated by bodies. Only animal bodies were visible at that era. California influence had not made itself felt and mohair and alpaca shrouded human form even at the beaches. Ladies were considered to be solid around the hem.

Four years of boarding school and another four of college taught me a good deal more about people and the shapes and sizes in which they grew, and I began drawing portraits in my spare time. Caesar's dull campaigns and the confusion of trigonometry reduced the spare time to a very small margin indeed, but I determined that when I had finished formal education I should go to art school and do what I had wanted to do all my life.

So I set to work in 1927 to become an artist in the Pennsylvania Academy of Fine Arts, where instruction kept well within the bounds of decorous caution.

At the end of my third year I had the honor to win one of the Cresson awards—traveling scholarships carrying a stipend of a thousand dollars. I also won a prize for the best drawings of animals made during the school year. The traveling scholarship I did not accept, for after three years of the Academy I was sick to death of art school art and wanted nothing but a summer of tennis and swimming in California.

In the fall I returned east, full of hope and sunburn, and started trying to make art pay, which it did though not much. I took every order that came along—posters, stencil designs for Italian restaurants, painted screens for sportsmen, portraits of horses in pastel and of children in bas-relief, commissions to design and make modern furniture and even an order for a tombstone. This varied work added nothing to modern American art, but taught me a great deal about working quickly and well in various materials.

In 1933 Buckminster Fuller, inventor of the Dymaxion house and co-inventor with Starling Burgess of the Dymaxion car, invited me to work in the Dymaxion factory.

There followed the most instructive and inventive six months of my life. The Dymaxion plant gave me exactly what I wanted, the things the Academy of Fine Arts could not give—that is, the principles of good workmanship. I think there are a great many "artists" but awfully few real craftsmen. Use of tools, and neat, fast, strong construction are not taught much in art schools.

It was in Dymaxion that I made my first experiments with abstract forms. Starling Burgess had a six foot model of the hull of one of his cup-defenders hanging in the office—a great, white, flying shape. It was one of the most beautiful things I had ever seen and awakened in me an interest in shape simply as shape. At this time I did the large bird-like form called *Cosmic Presence.*

Leaving the Dymaxion with a new knowledge of technique, particularly in working wood, and with a keener interest in everything, I worked four months for the P.W.A.P. making a set of illustrations for a book published by the Museum of Natural History and a bust of Horace Greeley for City College. During the course of the year I executed a number of small private commissions and exhibited work in the Architectural League of New York, the Woodstock Gallery, and the Pennsylvania Academy of Fine Arts Annual.

Then in the Spring of 1935 I went to Russia. I wanted to see how the artists were organized over there, how they were utilized in the scheme of life, and how socialized patronage affected the arts.

I found that from an economic-social standpoint the Soviet artist enjoys the happiest situation in the world: as a trade union member he enjoys protection and social security,

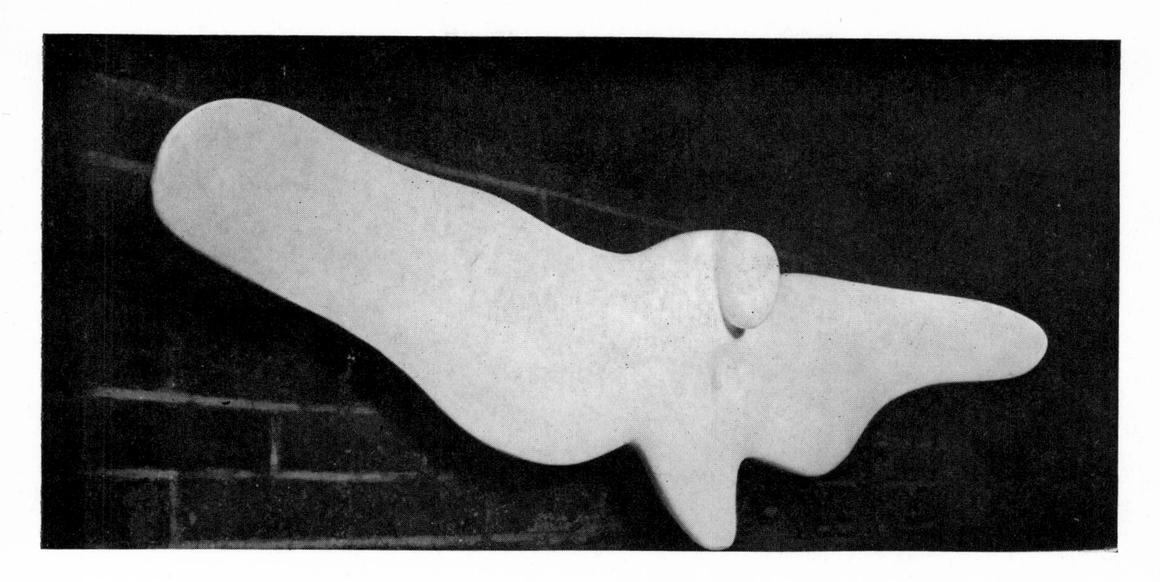

Emma Lu Davis. Cosmic Presence. 1934. Wood, 66″ long. Lent by Mrs. J. Rosenbaum.

he never lacks employment, and building and decorative projects are broad enough to include all varieties of work—except good work. This, I believe, was in no way the fault of socialism. Soviet artists are not regimented any more than artists in other countries, but it happens that the pressure of popular taste is toward bad and tawdry styles in painting and sculpture. Russia has not a broad or intelligent popular base of appreciation of beautiful projects. The Russian tradition of real folk painting disappeared four or five hundred years ago with the last of the fine ikons. Since then there has been nothing but a second-rate tradition of academic paint and clay pushing.

So present-day Soviet artists have every opportunity to go to town, but fail miserably because the cheap academic traditions have been continued under the name of "socialist realism"—that is, all the facts and none of the meaning of the subject.

Now I am chiefly concerned with the development of cooperative artist groups in America. I feel that cooperation within the craft and public patronage on a generous scale but not connected with relief are the hope of American artists. I like my own country and my craft, and I watch with satisfaction the growth of a self-conscious Americana and of a feeling of solidarity and social consciousness among American artists.

The years from 1938 until the summer of 1941 were spent as Artist in Residence at Reed College, Portland, Oregon. They were the most profitable and enjoyable three years

Emma Lu Davis. Black Bull. 1935. Wood, 34½″ high, 51″ long. Lent by Mrs. Walter Davenport, Winsted, Conn.

of my life. The students taught me how to look at art from the ordinary person's point of view, and also how to release the ordinary person's amazing creative ability. My latest work has been in Mexico City doing lithography and engraving with the boys of the Taller de Grafica.

Emma Lu Davis

Emma Lu Davis made a painted low-relief decoration for the Post Office at La Plata, Missouri, commissioned by the Section of Fine Arts of the Public Buildings Administration. She had a one-man exhibition in Peiping, China in 1937 at the Peiping Institute of Fine Arts. The Boyer Galleries in New York showed a group of her sculpture and drawings in 1937. She is represented in the collection of the Whitney Museum of American Art, New York.

Emma Lu Davis. Bantam Rooster. 1934. Painted wood with copper, 13¾″ high. Lent by the Whitney Museum of American Art, New York.

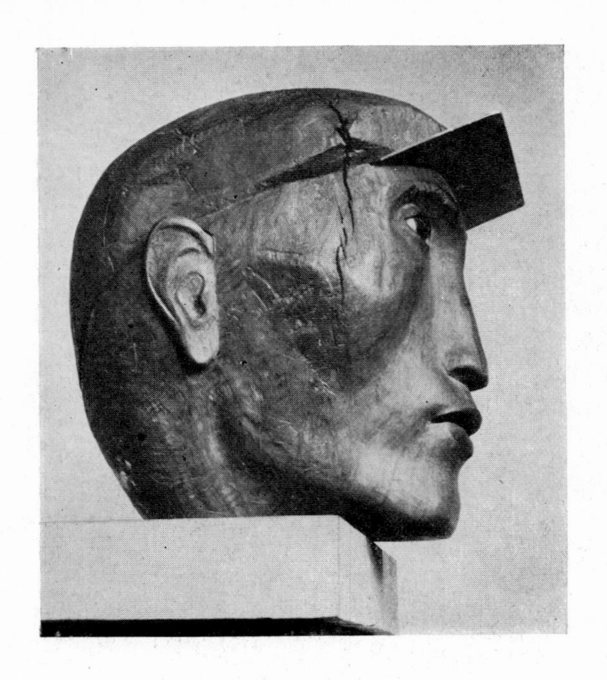

EMMA LU DAVIS. Hsiao Di-Di. 1936. Walnut, 6¾″ high. Lent by the artist.

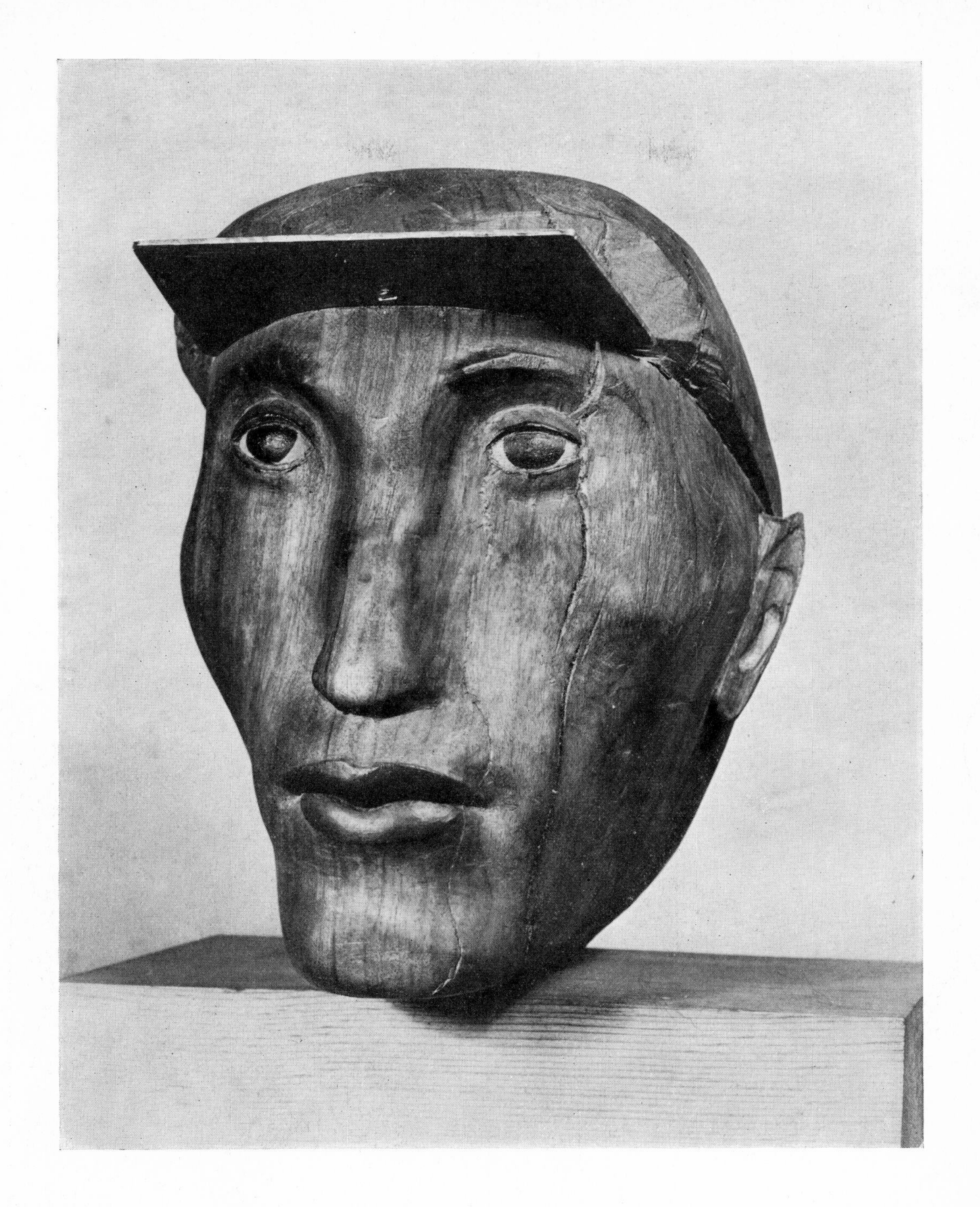

Emma Lu Davis. Head of Chinese Red Army Soldier. 1936. Walnut, 9¾″ high. Lent by Mrs. Jan de Graaff, Portland, Ore.

Emma Lu Davis. "Handies." 1939–41. Wood.

The artist says: "Handies" or hand sculpture are meant to be felt rather than looked at. They make an excellent substitute for cigarettes, chewing gum or doodling for those who tend to be fidgety in committee meetings. As an approach to abstract and unconventional sculpture they are an absolute find. People who wall their eyes and lay back their ears at visual abstracts will sit right down and make themselves at home with a "handy."

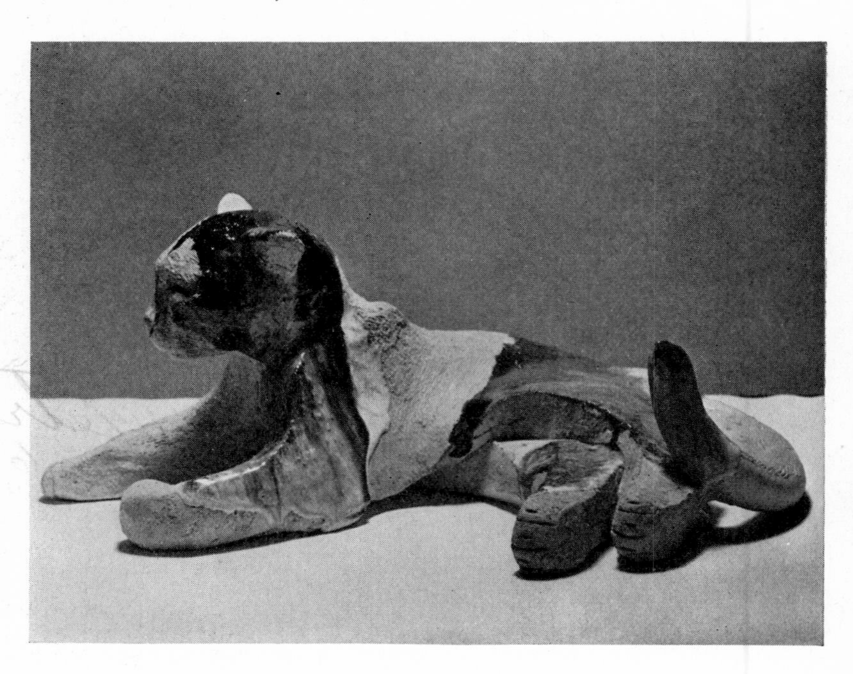

Emma Lu Davis. "Folded" Cat. 1941. Terra cotta, 18″ long.

"Folding" cats is a technique invented by the artist. She cuts a catskin shape out of clay and folds it into position, modeling only the head and tail.

MORRIS GRAVES

I paint to evolve a changing language of symbols, a language with which to remark upon the qualities of our mysterious capacities which direct us toward ultimate reality.

I paint to rest from the phenomena of the external world—to pronounce it—and to make notations of its essences with which to verify the inner eye.

MORRIS GRAVES

Morris Graves was born in Fox Valley, Oregon in August 1910. He has lived in western Washington since 1911. In 1930 he went to Japan, in 1940 to Puerto Rico. He lives at present in Seattle.

Graves has never had a one-man show. The Seattle Art Museum and the WPA Art Program, on which he worked for some time, own examples of his work.

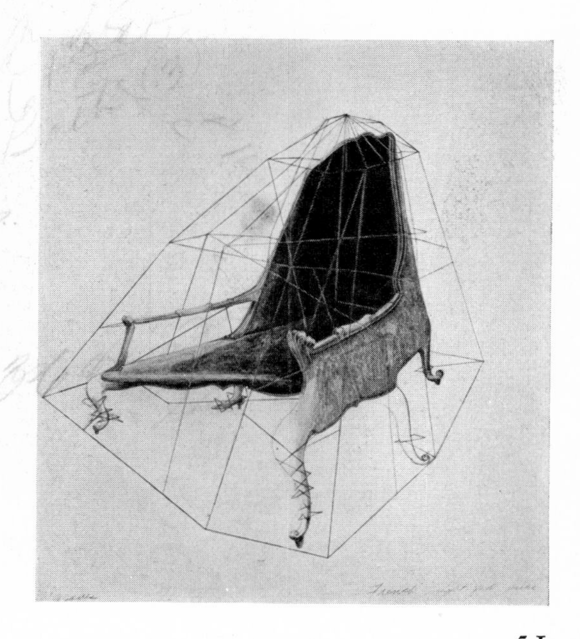

MORRIS GRAVES. French Nightfall Piece. One of a series in pencil and red ink, 26 x 21″. Lent by the artist.

MORRIS GRAVES. Constant Journey. Gouache, 12⅝ x 16⅛″. Lent by the artist.

MORRIS GRAVES. Message no. 6. One of a series, tempera and wax, 12 x 16½″. Lent by the WPA Art Program, Washington, D. C.

Morris Graves. Shore Birds. Gouache, 25⅞ x 28⅞". Lent by Lee Foley, Seattle.

Morris Graves. Bird Singing in the Moonlight. Gouache, 26¾ x 30⅛". Lent by the artist.

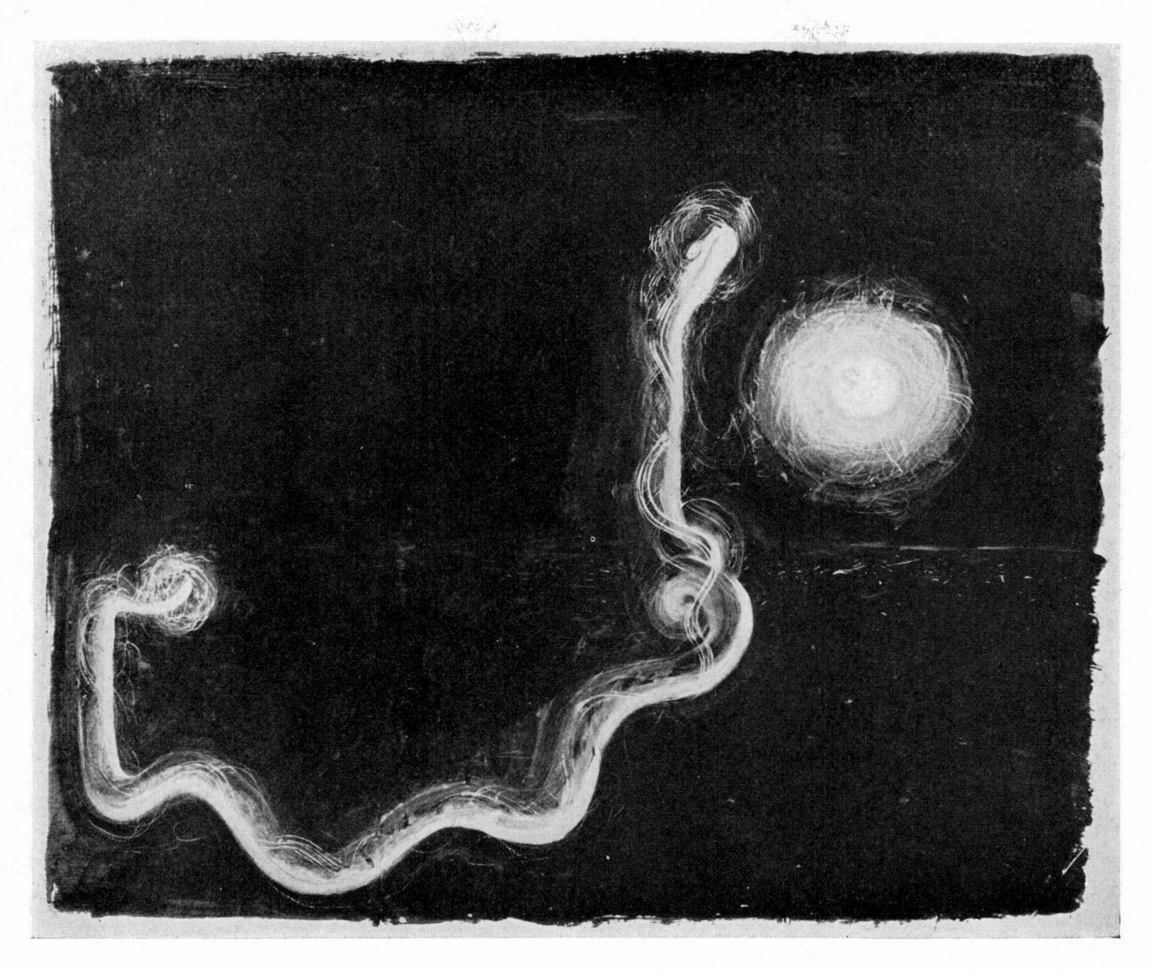

MORRIS GRAVES. Snake and Moon. Watercolor and gouache, 25½ x 30¼″. Lent by the artist.

MORRIS GRAVES. Little Known Bird of the Inner Eye. Gouache, 21 x 36¾″. Lent by the artist.

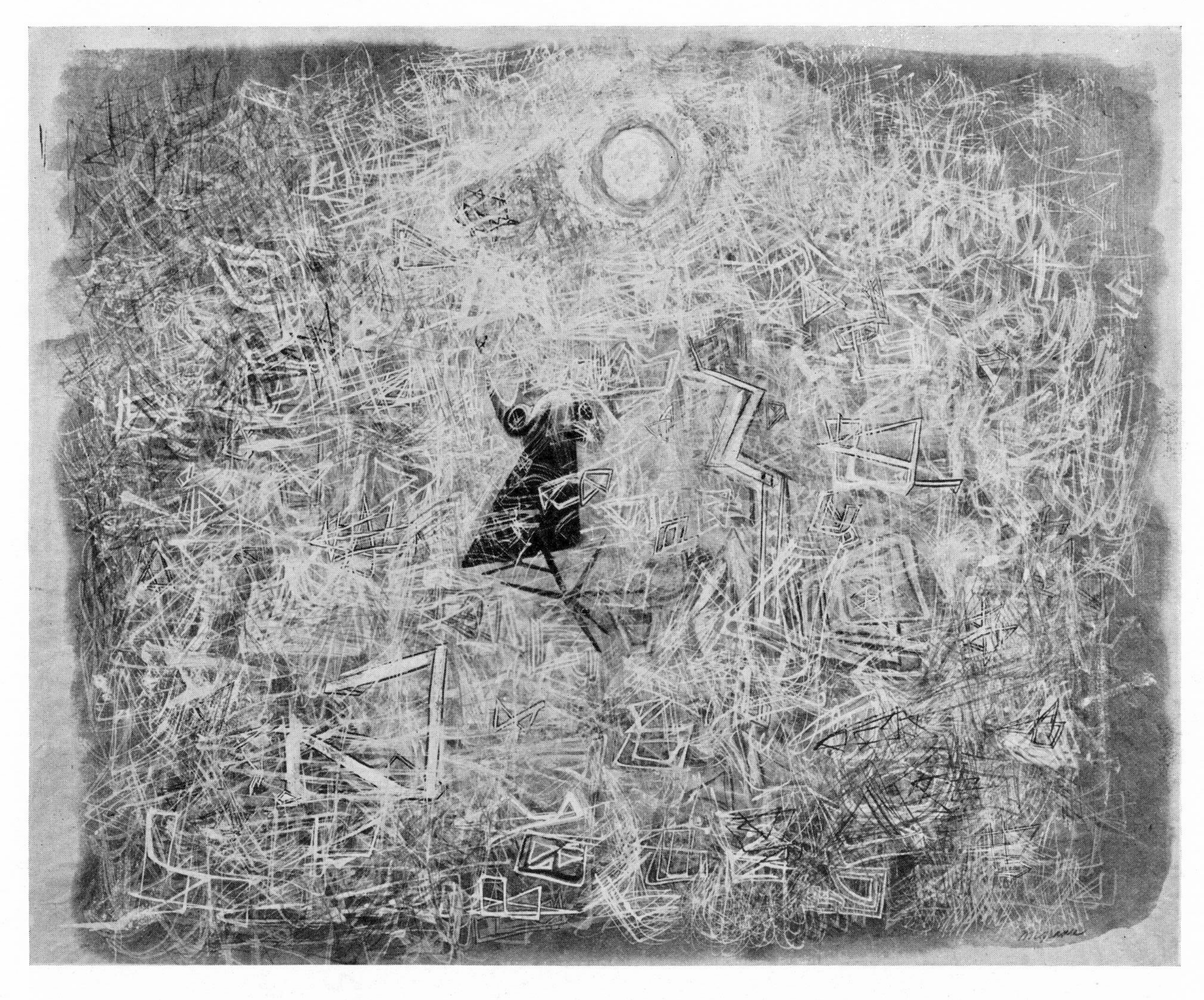

MORRIS GRAVES. Bird in the Moonlight. Gouache, 25 x 30¼". Lent by Mr. and Mrs. Charles Ross, Seattle.

Morris Graves. Purification. Series of nine gouaches, each 12½ x 16⅛″. Lent by the artist.

Morris Graves. Blind Bird. Gouache, 30⅛ x 27″. Lent by the artist.

JOSEPH HIRSCH

It's ten to one you know what art is, but maybe twenty to one you can't say it. If you are Philistine enough to ask "Well, what is the point in attempting to throw a phraseological lasso around art?" you've got me.

However, consider art *in relation to people* and you've got hold of something! That really calls for a lasso, today especially. As a blowing wind is visible only in its effects, so might we perceive art best in seeing what it does to people. Since a painting can be stimulating or depressing or entertaining only to the degree that those who look at it are so affected, the spectators therefore are undeniably elements in a creative work of art. Whatever intrinsic value we feel our picture may possess, it can have real value, can exert its influence or charm, can speak, only when it leaves the studio and goes out into the world. A gifted tongue is eloquent only when it is heard.

Now the *function* of art, Tolstoy once said, is "to infect others with the artist's world view." Does not any genuine personal expression, by its very nature, seek to propagandize? In my painting I want to castigate the things I hate and paint monuments to what I feel is noble. I want to talk and be heard. I want to disturb people who admit they know nothing about art, in as constructive a way as Picasso has disturbed the artists who felt they knew all about art. I want to take the stump for what I think is beautiful and important in this day.

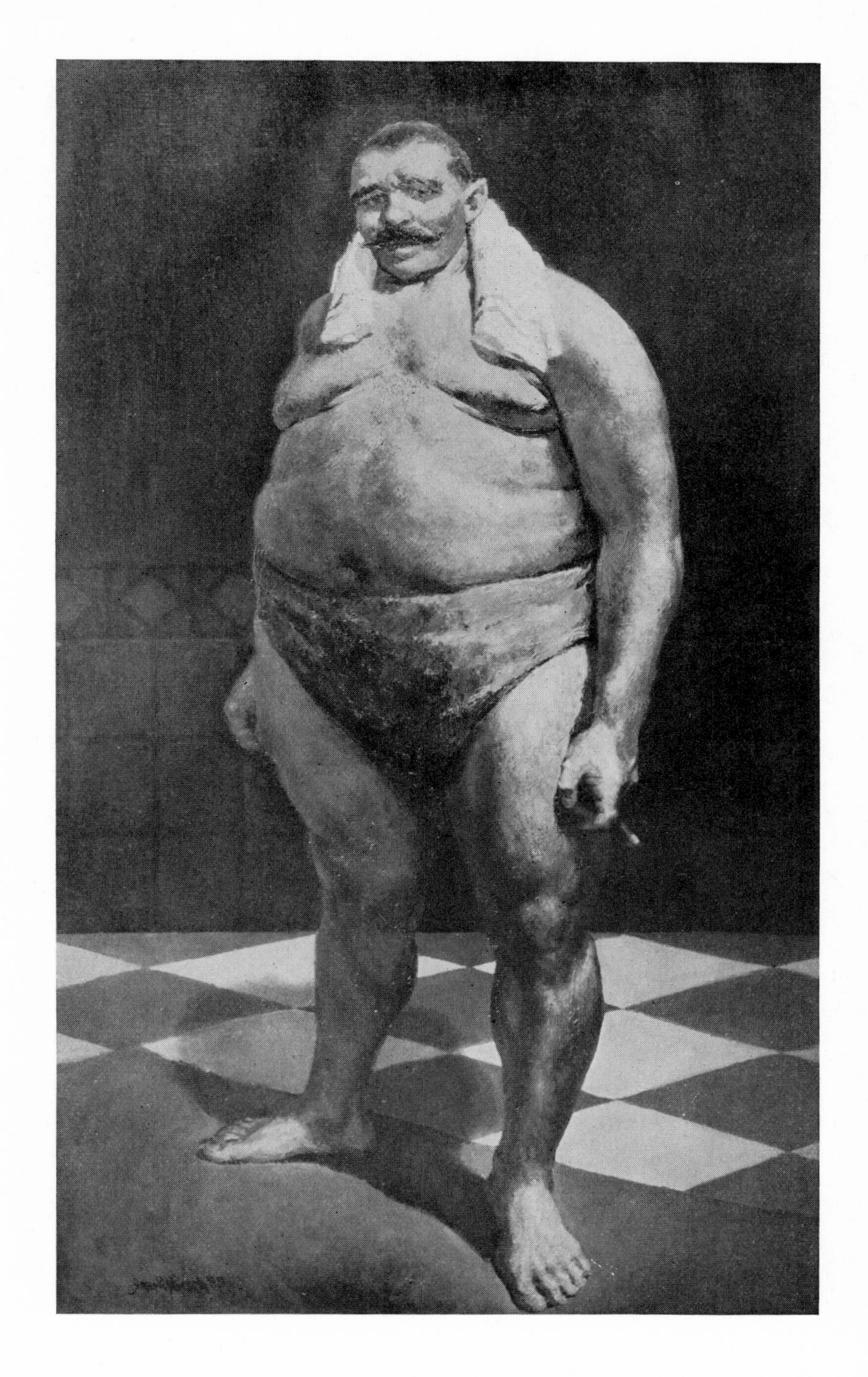

Joseph Hirsch. Masseur Tom. 1933. Oil on canvas, 80 x 47¼″. Lent by Associated American Artists, New York.

JOSEPH HIRSCH. Two Men. 1937. Oil on canvas, 18⅛ x 48¼″. The Museum of Modern Art, Mrs. John D. Rockefeller, Jr. Purchase Fund.

The great Paris school was properly part of a world of sunlight, where no one seems ever to have wept or starved; it was a joyous new adventure spurred on by the rich imaginations of the great post-impressionists. The weather has changed and, for all our nostalgia, the fruits of today are not odalisques nor pears and mandolin on a rumpled tablecloth. Ours is an era of accelerated transition, this is the season for weapons. The choice of whether to fight or escape is itself inescapable, in art as in everyday living, for in the very avoidance of making such a decision, paradoxically, one makes a choice. When the weather of his society proved stormy, the lesser artist has looked the other way or sought escape, while the great artist, as we know, has wielded his art as a magnificent weapon truly mightier than the sword. But whether the social climate of their times was calm or turbulent, the real men of art have invariably been keenly aware of the world about them. So it strikes me that a re-affirmation by today's sincere artist of his faith in the common ordinary man will be as natural as was, for example, the emphasis by El Greco, in his day, on his faith in the Church.

The cause of democracy is the cause of creative art, and the contemporary artist who cherishes his art freedom will accordingly fight for the democracy in which it flourishes. When the barometer rises again and the thunder fades away, the day shall dawn when all men will be free—yes, free to paint odalisques and pears and tablecloths to their hearts' content.

JOSEPH HIRSCH

JOSEPH HIRSCH. Landscape with Tear Gas. 1937. Oil on canvas, 23 x 31". Lent by Associated American Artists, New York.

Joseph Hirsch was born in Philadelphia in 1910. In 1928 he was awarded a four year scholarship at the Pennsylvania Museum School of Industrial Art, and in 1932 he studied with George Luks in New York. In 1935 he won the Woolley Fellowship of the Institute of International Education which enabled him to travel for a year and a half in Europe and the Orient.

While on the WPA Federal Art Project of Pennsylvania, Hirsch painted murals in the Benjamin Franklin High School, Philadelphia, in 1938. He has had three one-man shows—in 1937 at the A.C.A. Gallery, Philadelphia, in 1941 at the Carlen Galleries, Philadelphia, and at the Amalgamated Meatcutters Union in New York. At the exhibition *American Art Today* at the New York World's Fair 1939, Hirsch's painting *Two Men* (see page 62) won a popular ballot of 120,000 votes for "best painting" in the show. He is represented in the collections of the Addison Gallery of American Art, Andover, the Museum of Modern Art, New York, and the Philadelphia Museum of Art.

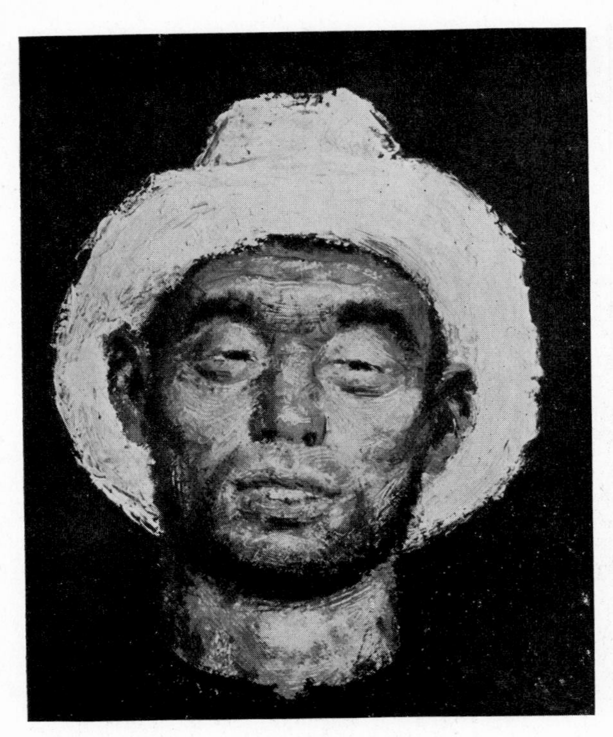

Joseph Hirsch. Chinese-American. 1941. Oil on panel, 10 x 8″. Lent by Associated American Artists, New York.

Joseph Hirsch. The Confidence. 1941. Oil on canvas, 14 x 18″. Lent by Samuel Spewack, New Hope, Pa.

Joseph Hirsch. The Drink. 1941. Oil on canvas, 13 x 23″. Lent by Mr. and Mrs. Benjamin Laskin, Germantown, Pa.

Joseph Hirsch. Vermont Roof. 1940. Oil on canvas, 10¼ x 24½″. Lent by Associated American Artists, New York.

Joseph Hirsch. The Warrior. 1940. Oil on canvas, 32 x 18″.
Lent by Associated American Artists, New York.

DONAL HORD

The artist in this, the extreme southwestern, corner of the United States lives in an environment that is concerned less with people and an industrialized landscape than with the strong light beating on ancient, granitic, and sparsely watered hills. Each year the question of seasonal rains affects the land. Will the dams overflow, or will it be necessary to graze cattle on the little patches of green in the reservoir basins? Will there be enough water? That is in essence the background of this region which runs diagonally north through Nevada and east through and beyond Arizona—and south into Mexico. For this is on the border of what botanists call the Sonora Zone. If an artist lives here long enough and knows the dry, boulder-studded reaches of the American deserts, he becomes affected by that same symbolism of forces, rather than by an impact of personalities, that affected the ancient Asiatics who passed through here on their way south to develop art in Mexico.

I have lived in the Southwest most of my life. I once spent fourteen months in Mexico and thereafter eight months in New York and Philadelphia. Both these cities seemed, and still seem, more foreign to me than the Mexican states south of our border. Feeling this, I came home.

A section of this article is reprinted by permission of the *Spanish Village Art Quarterly*.

I learned to model and carve here in southern California where sunlight is intense and shadows are harsh. Very few western sculptors south of San Francisco were carving at that time. I learned and broke the maxim: "Never use anything but a chisel on wood." I have riffled wood, I have sanded and polished wood, and polychromed and laid metal leaf over it. From many mistakes one learns many things. I learned direct carving.

Granite of fine quality is available here, black diorite, green diorite, obsidian and felsite. Granite is a tough stone to crush into forms. Our diorite rings like an anvil and gives tactile pleasure after its dark crystals have been rubbed smooth. The *Aztec*, my second stone figure, was beaten from this material. It was shaped in the open, under all lights and conditions, and after seven months of struggle with peen and bouchard hammers, modern air tools and diamond points were brought into use.

A sculptor's approach to his art is conditioned by the materials he favors.

Stone sculpture and clay modeling have little in common. Clay seems to me a negative material, a substance of trial and error, addition and subtraction, fleeting emotion. It is a practice medium in which ideas may be evolved, to be, more often than not, made permanent in metal or marble.

Stone in the carver's vocabulary does not mean limestone, marble, alabaster, sandstone nor Caen stone. These so-called stones are easier to work than wood. They may be filed and sandpapered, and generally are, into soft nuances of form and texture. Granite, diorite, porphyry and basalt are austere, intractable materials, tight grained and rich in tone. These are positive materials and the sculptor must be fully cognizant of their rigid limitations before he decides what formal shape may be imposed upon them.

Stone teaches one thing to the artist—that agonies and fears and posturings should not be beaten into a boulder that has kinship only with serene eternity. Stone sculpture should not carry a shape foreign to the spirit of timelessness.

The actual physical execution of sculpture in hard stone is long and arduous. Its shaping is timed by months rather than by days. Obsidian, diorite, granite, check off years; limestone and marble, months; clay, days and weeks.

A monolith is brought from the quarry. The blacksmith sharpens and tempers a pile of points while the stone is studied. The rough proportions were decided long before the stone was purchased, but now the stone envelops the idea and must be forced to yield it. The attack is begun with heavy steel points and a three-pound hammer. The forge is never idle while this work goes on.

The air hammer was unknown in Egypt and during the Renaissance. One wonders what statues might have been carved had it been available. This hammer, air driven, holds the shank of a diamond point—a four or nine pointed tool that pulverizes the stone surface. This tool actually develops the forms and must be used carefully to avoid bruising or fracturing the stone. The final work is done with chisels, easing out little forms and making minor adjustments that immediately precede weeks of grinding with carborundum stones until the crushed crystals are removed and the unblemished stone revealed. It would be a pleasure to state that this is the sculpture as the public will see it—but more often than not the polish is chiseled away again because certain forms gain undue prominence apparent only under the unrestrained play of light.

Sculpture should be carved in the full ever-changing sunlight possible in our climate. Anyone can discover that a form intended to be viewed in an outdoor light should be created under identical circumstances—turned in the direction that the sculpture will eventually face.

DONAL HORD

Donal Hord was born in 1902 at Prentice, Wisconsin. He went to live in San Diego in 1916. From 1926 to 1928 he attended the Santa Barbara School of Fine Arts, studying modeling and lost-wax casting under Archibald Dawson of Glasgow. An exchange scholarship enabled him to go to Mexico in 1928 and later to Philadelphia, where he worked briefly at the Pennsylvania Academy; and to New York, where, he says, he was "overwhelmed by the Museum of Natural History."

Since 1930 Hord has lived and worked in San Diego, devoting himself to stone and wood carving. From 1936 through 1941 the WPA Art Program sponsored Hord's major work, the *Aztec* (see page 71) for the campus of the San Diego State College, the *Guardian of Water*, a fourteen-foot fountain figure in diorite for the Civic Center of San Diego, and the *Legend of California*, a monumental series of seven reliefs in Indiana limestone for the façade of the high school library in Coronado, California.

Hord has never had a one-man exhibition. He is represented in the collection of the San Diego Fine Arts Society.

Donal Hord. Back view and detail of head of The Aztec.

Donal Hord. The Aztec. 1936–37. Diorite, 52″ high. Lent by the San Diego State College, through the Southern California WPA Art Program, Los Angeles.

Donal Hord. Mexican Mother and Child. 1938. Tennessee marble, 16¾″ high. Lent by the Franklin D. Roosevelt Library, Hyde Park, through the WPA Art Program, Washington, D. C.

Donal Hord. Mexican Beggar. 1938. Columbia marble, 12¾″ high. Lent by the WPA Art Program, Washington, D. C.

DONAL HORD. Veiled Figure. 1938. Tennessee marble, 15¼" high. Lent by the WPA Art Program, Washington, D. C.

CHARLES HOWARD

I had the experience, sometime early in the 1920's, of seeing a painting which made me realize that the thing I most wanted to do was to paint. The picture was by Giorgione. The place a little town in the hinterland of Venice. I've forgotten now the circumstances of my state of mind at the time, as well as the name of the picture, yet today no impression is so strong as it was then. Quite possibly such an experience is not unusual, but for me it was the beginning.

I have attended no art schools as such. I learned to handle paint in a decorating shop run by Louis Bouché and Rudolph Guertler in New York. I worked there for about five years. I was lucky in the association: wide knowledge, awareness, sensibility, sound craftsmanship and friendship were the developing influences. I thought it was the best way at the time and I continue to think so.

I have welcomed the influence of other painters. I don't believe in pure originality, and in the elaboration of my work I have relied upon my own obsession. If that weren't strong enough to integrate its own expression, it seems to me it would be no use painting anyway.

Generally speaking, the subject matter of the paintings is derived from everyday objects. A stone, a bird, a lamp post often serve as well as anything else. As the painter

Charles Howard. Generation. 1940. Oil on canvas, 15⅛ x 18″. Lent by the artist.

of the pictures, I operate as the dramatizing agent. The intention is to recall the shapes and relations of things which are common to all mankind. I consider that this is the object of all artists and that whatever else intervenes in a picture is merely arbitrary.

The titles appended to these pictures are supplementary and allusive. They have no other function.

Charles Howard

Charles Howard was born in Montclair, New Jersey in 1899 and grew up in Berkeley, California, graduating from the University of California in 1921. He started to paint in 1924, following two years' sojourn in France and Italy.

CHARLES HOWARD. The Cage. 1938. Gouache, 21⅛ x 29⅛″. Lent by the artist.

From 1926 through 1931 Howard worked as a journeyman painter and designer in the decorating shop of Louis Bouché and Rudolph Guertler in New York City. Since 1930 he has done a number of mural decorations, among them the De La Warr Pavilion at Bexhill, Sussex, England, in association with Edward Wadsworth. During the past year, under the California WPA Art Program, he has designed abstract mural decorations for the United States Naval Air Station, Alameda, California.

Following a one-man show at the Julien Levy Gallery in New York in 1933, Howard went to England where he remained until 1940. He had one-man shows at the Bloomsbury and Guggenheim Jeune Galleries in London in 1935 and 1939, and showed in group exhibitions in London, Amsterdam, Paris, Montreal, São Paulo (Brazil), San Francisco, Honolulu and Tokyo. He was associated with the Surrealist group in London from 1936 to 1938. Since May 1940 he has lived in San Francisco, where he had a one-man show at the Courvoisier Gallery in 1941.

Charles Howard. Trinity. 1941. Oil on canvas, 24⅛ x 34¼″. Lent by the artist.

RICO LEBRUN

I have never been able to discover for myself the actual reason for the implied divorce between pure draughtsmanship and pure painting. To me this is not only unfeeling but utterly incomprehensible.

The science of drawing has been at the core of the most aloof theorems of Uccello, as well as at the heart of the passionate baroque of El Greco. Drawing describes the content of the times in its resilience of contour. The contour is often the catalyst.

In its deepest sense of expression, color is plastic drawing. There is no compromise of meaning. But there have been masterly re-definitions. From Rembrandt to Picasso, Mantegna to Rouault, the answer is always painting with drawing and full color with line and within plane.

For me the aim is to participate in the living world of all peoples—to grasp this, its significance, and forge it, draw it, illustrate and give it in terms understandable and, I hope, acceptable to them.

RICO LEBRUN

RICO LEBRUN. Migration to Nowhere. 1941. Gouache on board, 30 x 48″. Lent by the artist.

Rico Lebrun was born in Naples, Italy in 1900. He was trained in banking. He started drawing and painting by himself very early, and while attending technical schools he studied in night classes at the Naples Academy of Arts.

He served in the Italian army during the World War. After his discharge from the army he went to work in a stained glass factory in Naples. In 1924 he came to America to establish a branch factory in Springfield, Illinois. A year later he moved to New York, following a number of trades and trying to keep up his painting.

Lebrun was granted a Guggenheim fellowship in 1935–36 and a renewal in 1937–38. Commissioned by the Section of Fine Arts of the Public Buildings Administration, he painted frescoes for the New York City Post Office Annex. He has taught at the Art Students' League in New York and at the Chouinard Art Institute in Los Angeles. For the past two years he has lived and worked in Santa Barbara, California.

Lebrun has never had a one-man exhibition although he has been represented in group exhibitions in various museums. Examples of his work are owned by the Wadsworth Atheneum in Hartford and the Santa Barbara Museum of Art.

RICO LEBRUN. A Penny. 1941. Oil and tempera on board, 19 x 24″. Lent by the artist.

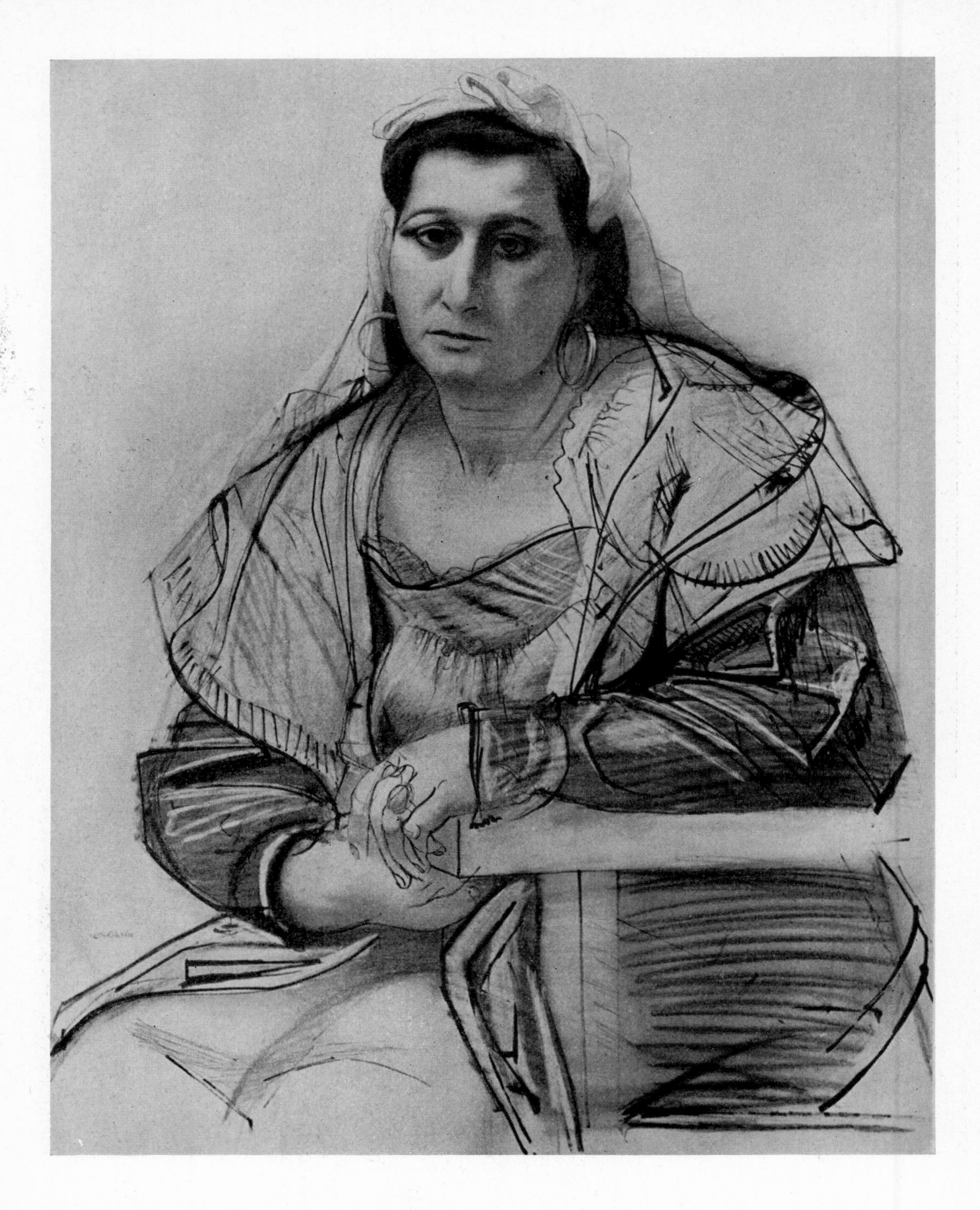

Rico Lebrun. Ortensia. 1941. Ink and chalk on board, 40 x 30″. Lent by George P. Raymond, New York.

Rico Lebrun. Seated Clown. 1941. Ink and chalk on board, 40 x 30″. Lent by the Santa Barbara Museum of Art.

Rico Lebrun. The Relatives of San Gennaro. 1941. Ink, 6½ x 8¼″. Lent by the artist.

Rico Lebrun. The Ragged One. 1941. Ink and chalk, 25 x 19″. Lent by the artist.

RICO LEBRUN. Bather. 1940. Oil on canvas, 50 x 30″. Lent by the artist.

JACK LEVINE

Essentially a city dweller, I find that the aspects of man and his environment in a large city are all I need to work with. I find my approach to painting inseparable from my approach to the world. Justice is more important than good looks. The artist must sit in judgment and intelligently evaluate the case for any aspect of the world he deals with. The validity of his work will rest on the humanity of his decision. A painting is good for the very same reason that anything in this world is good.

I feel the sordid neglect of a slum section strongly enough to wish to be a steward of its contents, to enumerate its increment—newspaper, cigarette butts, torn posters, empty match cards, broken bottles, orange rinds, overflowing garbage cans, flies, boarded houses, gas lights, and so on—to present this picture in the very places where the escapist plans his flight.

It has been an idiosyncrasy of mine to argue that a man so overtaxed in working for another man that he defeats his own cause, is not his own man. This I accept for myself as the reason why, to me, the symbol of work can never express the working man. The picture I persist in painting is an evening scene, designed to catch the man *not* at work, tired and overwhelmed but still, for the time, a free man. The consciousness that may be projected by the limpidness of an eye or a gentle incertitude of gesture is as far as I go in putting my characters into action, because of some logic of the psychological approach. Movement in my canvases embraces every object as well as atmosphere. Dramatic action on the part of the characters is latent. I distort images in an attempt to weld the drama of man and his environment.

That part of my work which is satirical is based on observations gathered in countless hours, hanging around street corners and cafeterias. There I often hear from urbane and case-hardened cronies about crooked contractors, ward heelers, racketeers, minions of the law and the like. It is my privilege as an artist to put these gentlemen on trial, to give them every ingratiating characteristic they might normally have, and then present them, smiles, benevolence and all, in my own terms.

If my frosty old gentleman in evening clothes beams with his right eye and has a cold fishy stare in his left, that is not an accident. If a policeman reposefully examines a hangnail, that is not necessarily the sum total of his activity. In this case it is an enforced genre to familiarize the spectator with the officer, to point out that he, too, has his cares and woes.

The mechanism is one of playing a counter-aspect against the original thesis, leaving it up to the spectator to judge the merits of the case. My experience is that generally the thesis is readily understood.

I paint the poor and the rich, in different pictures, and give them different treatment. I think this is as it should be.

JACK LEVINE

In 1939 Jack Levine wrote: Born in Boston, 1915; youngest of family of eight. Began drawing very young. Attended children's classes at a community center. When I was eight, my family moved from the slum-ridden South End to Roxbury, throttling residential suburb. Horrified by the trees and piazzas, I consoled myself by making drawings of drunkards and other things I remembered. Later went to classes at the Boston Museum, and tried to draw like Leonardo, di Credi, Crivelli, Mantegna, etc. Attracted the attention of Dr. Denman Ross, eminent collector and theorist, and studied with him. He expounded the impressionist approach to representation, made representation a matter of arithmetical accuracy. His teaching helped me, but I have never since resorted to his method or esthetic. I was then about eighteen. A year later I was on the WPA Art Project. Thus subsidized, I speedily re-evaluated all my ideas. Decided to paint what I knew best and had known longest.

Jack Levine had a one-man exhibition at the Downtown Gallery, New York in 1939.

Jack Levine. The Street. 1938. Oil tempera and oil on canvas, 60 x 84″. Lent by the WPA Art Program, Washington, D. C.

JACK LEVINE. The Millionaire. 1938. Oil on canvas, 34 x 16″. Lent by David L. Podell, New York.

JACK LEVINE. The Feast of Pure Reason. 1937. Oil on canvas, 42 x 48″. Lent by the WPA Art Program, Washington, D. C.

JACK LEVINE. Planning Solomon's Temple. 1941. Oil on composition board, 10 x 8". Lent by Herman Shulman, New York.

JACK LEVINE. Card Game. 1941. Oil on canvas, 16 x 14". Lent by Mr. and Mrs. Samuel A. Lewisohn, New York.

JACK LEVINE. The Banquet. 1941. Oil on canvas, 25¼ x 30″. Lent by the Downtown Gallery, New York.

HELEN LUNDEBERG

I was born in Chicago in 1908. Since the age of four I have lived and worked in southern California. In 1930 I received an art scholarship which permitted me to work and study for three years under the guidance of Lorser Feitelson. I have been actively associated with Lorser Feitelson in the development and exposition of Postsurrealism since its origin in California in 1934.

I am, apparently, a classicist by nature as well as conviction. By classicism I mean, not traditionalism of any sort, but a highly conscious concern with esthetic structure which is the antithesis of intuitive, romantic, or realistic approaches to painting. My aim, realized or not, is to calculate, and reconsider, every element in a painting with regard to its function in the whole organization. That, I believe, is the classic attitude.

In contrast to the surrealist program of intuitive expression and subconscious automatic recordings, Postsurrealism explores the field of psychological science to create a classic subjective expression. The pictorial elements are deliberately arranged to stimulate, in the mind of the spectator, an ordered, pleasurable, introspective activity, resulting in a configuration, or subjective unity, which *is* the esthetic order of the painting and which makes possible the long-discussed ideal integrity of subject matter and form.

HELEN LUNDEBERG

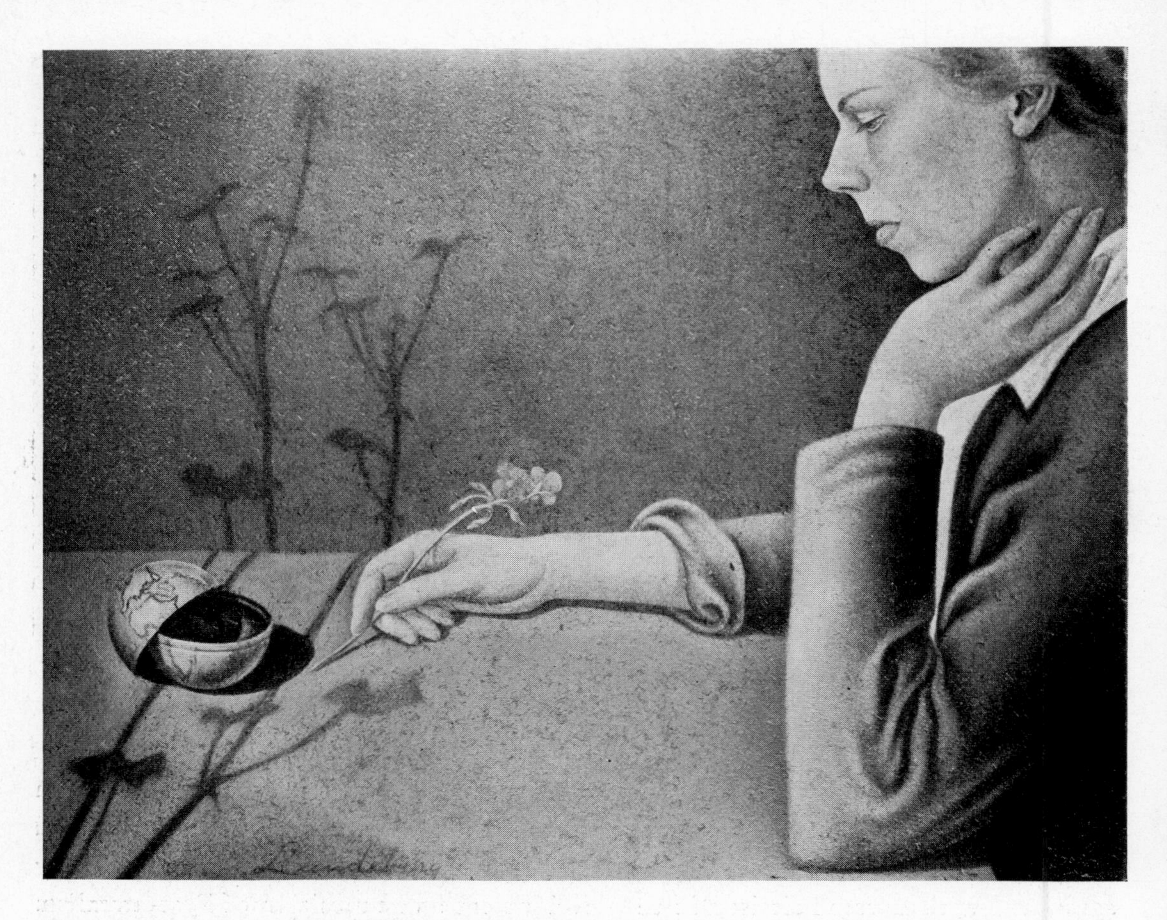

HELEN LUNDEBERG. Artist, Flower and Hemispheres. 1934. Oil on celotex, 23¾ x 30″. Lent by the San Francisco Museum of Art.

Helen Lundeberg has been working for several years as a mural designer on the WPA Art Program in southern California. Although she has never had a one-man exhibition she showed about a dozen of her paintings with the Postsurrealist group in 1936 at the San Francisco Museum of Art and at the Brooklyn Museum, New York.

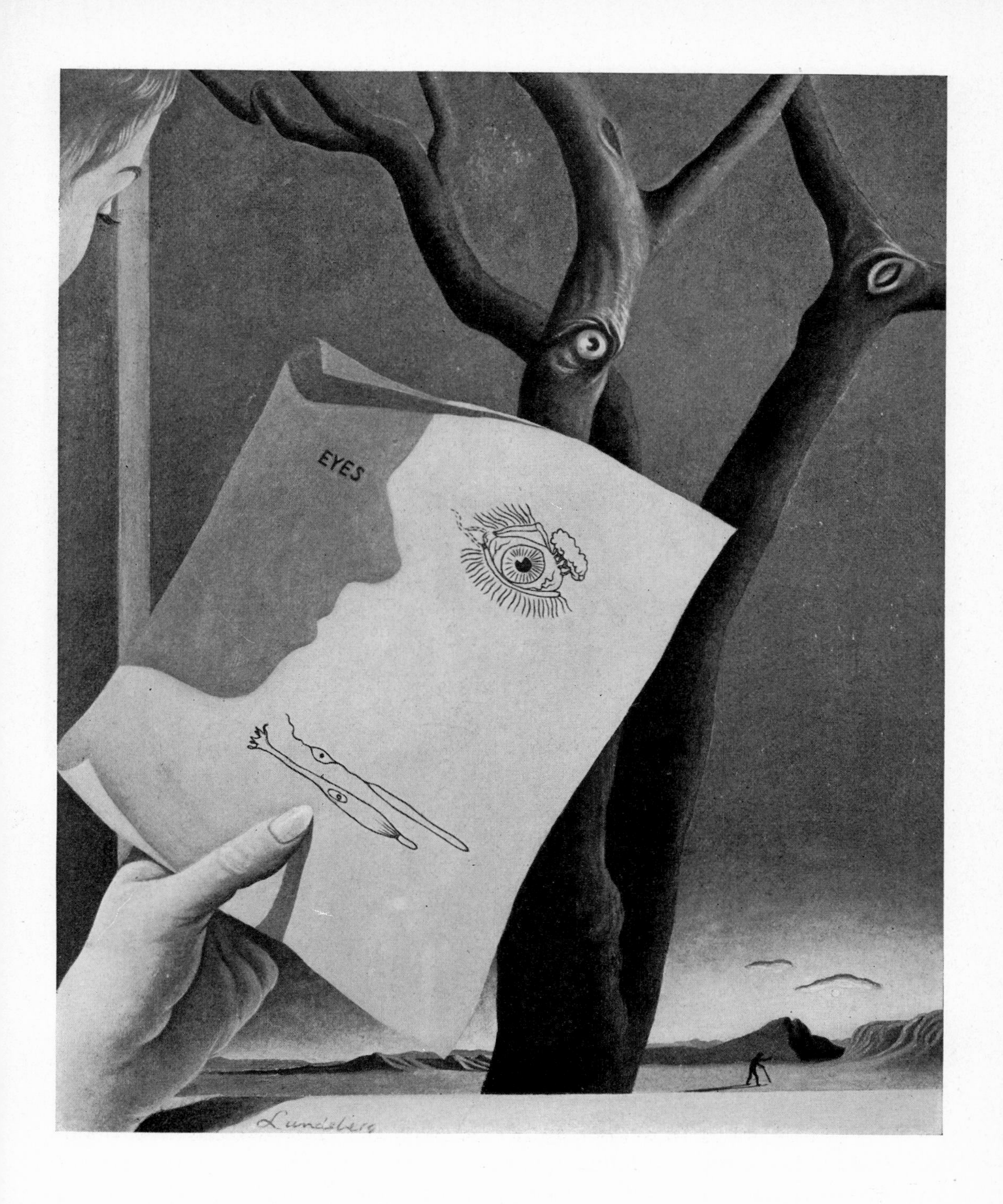

Helen Lundeberg. Eyes. 1938–39. Oil on masonite, 16 x 13¼″. Lent by the artist.

Helen Lundeberg. The Tree. 1938. Oil on masonite, 30½ x 24″. Lent by the artist.

FLETCHER MARTIN

I am practically self-taught, but the only real difference that makes is that I had to learn the same lessons in a different way—by making a pest of myself with my painter friends, watching (in the very beginning) everybody I could find who made things with a brush, from sign painters on up, and by looking at all the pictures and reproductions I could find. Now that I teach other students I am inclined to think that the really good ones, by their curiosity and intelligent skepticism, get their art education much the same way except that there is someone always present who is supposed to know a lot of the answers.

If I have a preference for any medium it is drawing. Of course drawing problems are present in all media but I mean drawing for its own sake. If I could afford to collect anything by the big boys it would be their drawings.

When I have a subject in mind for a painting I always make a number of linear abstract designs based on the material of my subject. When this pleases me as pure design I draw on the canvas with the brush and thin color, setting in these abstract lines, and then develop the form contours around them. From that beginning I proceed with the development in form and color. I guess I work rather fast. Never more than ten days on an easel picture.

Anything within our ken, I think, is possible material for a good picture, whether it be an idea, an experience or some object. The most commonplace subject need not be a commonplace picture.

The painter who means most to me is Cézanne.

It may be fortunate for me that I was never able to go to Europe because impressions and experiences mean a lot to me and they might have been the wrong kind for my particular way of working. Nearly all my subject material is a revived memory. I rarely make sketches of things which impress me until some time after the event. I think the time lapse helps me to be more selective as regards the material I want to use in the composition.

FLETCHER MARTIN

Fletcher Martin was born at Palisade, Colorado in 1904, son of a country newspaper editor. His family moved to Idaho when he was six and he spent most of his time on a ranch there until 1922. After working as harvest hand, lumberjack and construction worker in the northwest, he joined the Navy in 1922. Paid off in 1926, he settled in Los Angeles with a job in the printing business which he held for nine years, attending art lectures at night. About 1927 he had started to draw and paint in his spare time, and later he assisted a muralist and became interested in print making.

In 1935 the WPA Federal Art Project gave him an opportunity to devote all his time to painting. For the Project he painted murals in the North Hollywood High School. In 1937 he won a Section of Fine Arts competition for murals in the San Pedro (California) Post Office, and he has also decorated the Post Office at Lamesa, Texas.

Martin taught painting at the University of Iowa in 1940–41. He now holds the post of chairman of painting and drawing at the Kansas City Art Institute.

Martin had his first one-man show at the San Diego Fine Arts Gallery in 1933. Later one-man exhibitions were held at the Los Angeles Museum in 1939 and at the Midtown Galleries, New York, in 1940 and 1941. He is represented in the collections of the Los Angeles Museum, the Kansas City Art Institute, the Metropolitan Museum of Art and the Museum of Modern Art in New York.

FLETCHER MARTIN. Trouble in Frisco. 1938. Oil on canvas, 30 x 36″. The Museum of Modern Art, Mrs. John D. Rockefeller, Jr. Purchase Fund.

FLETCHER MARTIN. Out at Home. 1940. Oil on canvas, 23 x 44″. Lent by the Midtown Galleries, New York.

FLETCHER MARTIN. Temptation in Tonopah. 1940. Oil on wood, 18 x 12″. Lent by Mrs. Stanley Resor, Greenwich, Conn.

FLETCHER MARTIN. Stormy Weather. 1941. Oil on canvas, 40 x 24″. Lent by the Midtown Galleries, New York.

OCTAVIO MEDELLIN

I believe that sincere art must be elemental and close to the earth—a symbol of the people.

The trend of my art is toward the common people and everyday life, the kind of people and environment I myself come from. It is entirely away from politics and sophisticated ideas.

I think, as did the prehispanic and colonial Indian sculptors, that carving directly in stone is the only way to reach massive, round, and definite forms.

Stone is beautiful in itself and does not admit of any tricks. It makes one desire to bend its hard surface into form but not to take advantage of and destroy its character.

All the stone used in my work comes from Texas quarries. Some pieces are carved in limestone from quarries located near Austin, Texas. A very compact, semi-hard stone, it gives a beautiful texture when carved. I also use a rose-colored sandstone from west Texas. In color and grain it is similar to petrified wood and has a very special quality. I have also used a gray sandstone from southwest Texas, a hard stone that must be treated in a rough, coarse way.

OCTAVIO MEDELLIN

Octavio Medellin was born on May 23, 1908 in Matehuala, San Luis Potosí, Mexico, of Otomi Indian stock. He is a naturalized American citizen.

In 1921 his mother brought him and four brothers to the United States and they settled in San Antonio, Texas. Medellin attended night classes from 1925 to 1928 at the San Antonio Art School under José Arpa and Xavier Gonzalez, studying drawing and experimenting with wood sculpture. In 1928 he went to Chicago where he spent eighteen months studying life drawing at the Art Institute. He made a trip to Mexico in 1930, meeting Mexican artists, traveling in many states and living in small Indian villages along the Gulf of Mexico.

In 1931 Medellin was back in the United States, starting to carve directly in stone. During the next half-dozen years he completed a number of pieces of sculpture including several small commissions. Intensive study, for several months in 1938, of the ruins of the Maya temple of Chichén Itzá in Yucatán gave new impetus to Medellin's stone carving.

He has been teaching since 1939, first in San Antonio at the Art School of the Witte Memorial Museum and at the Villita Art Gallery, and for the past year at the North Texas State Teachers' College at Denton. The Witte Museum gave him a one-man show of sixteen pieces in 1938.

OCTAVIO MEDELLIN. Penitentes. 1940. Cast stone, 21¾" high. Lent by the artist.

OCTAVIO MEDELLIN. At the Stake. 1938. Wood, 21″ high. Lent by the artist.

OCTAVIO MEDELLIN. Holy Roller. 1941. Red terra cotta, 22″ high. Lent by Vladimir Golschmann, St. Louis.

OCTAVIO MEDELLIN. Primitive Woman. 1935. White limestone, 25¼″ high. Lent by the artist.

Octavio Medellin. Waiting Figure. 1940. Red sandstone, 23″ high. Lent by Mr. and Mrs. Frank Rosengren, San Antonio, Texas.

KNUD MERRILD

I am striving for that beauty of which Plato speaks, "not beautiful relatively, like other things, but always and naturally and absolutely." I shall, of course, never know if I attain this, but perhaps what Lawrence says is true: "The value of a picture lies in the esthetic emotion it brings, exactly as if it were a flower. Pictures are strange things, most of them die as sure as flowers die."

I pray I may succeed in enriching life, be it even for a few, and give a moment's pleasure. I shall not have worked in vain but have been amply rewarded.

KNUD MERRILD

Knud Merrild was born in 1894 in the east of Jutland, Denmark. At fourteen he was apprenticed to a house painter, with a promise from his father that he would help him to become an artist at the end of the four year period. After three and a half years he went to Copenhagen to start his art training. During the student years which followed he supported himself as a house painter and decorator.

In 1913 he worked in Sweden, and in 1914 in Germany. During the war he remained in Denmark attending the arts and crafts school, from which he was expelled in 1916 for his "extreme views on modern art." In 1918, after a brief period of study at the Royal Academy of Fine Arts, a travel stipend from the Danish government permitted him to go to Norway, Sweden and England. In order to stay on in England he worked at all sorts of jobs, and in 1921 left for America, remembering that the Danish critic, Georg Brandes, had said that America would be the future art center of the world.

Merrild and another Danish artist, K. G. Gotzsche, did commercial work together in New York for about a year. Then he and Gotzsche started for the west. At Taos they met D. H. Lawrence and spent a number of months with him and his wife—a period recorded in Merrild's book, *A Poet and Two Painters*, published in 1939. Merrild then went on to Los Angeles where he has lived ever since, except for trips to Europe in 1926 and 1938.

Merrild still supports himself chiefly as a house painter, producing his art in his spare time. He has had several one-man exhibitions in southern California, as well as at the San Francisco Museum of Art in 1937 and at the Boyer Galleries in Philadelphia and New York in 1937 and 1939. He is represented in the collections of the Los Angeles Museum and the Fine Arts Society of San Diego.

KNUD MERRILD. Synthesis. *c.* 1936. Gesso-wax, 10 x 9¼″. The Museum of Modern Art, Mrs. John D. Rockefeller, Jr. Purchase Fund.

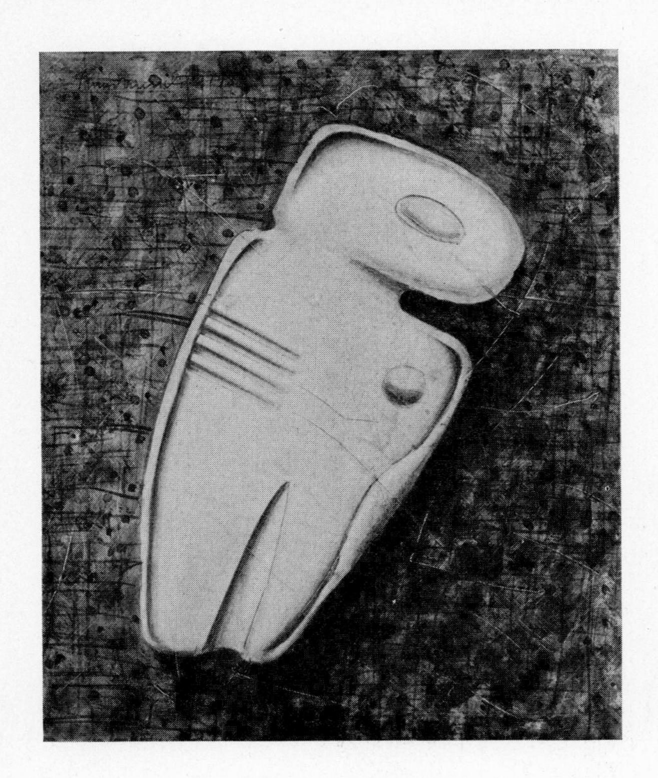

KNUD MERRILD. Herma. 1935. Gesso-wax, 10½ x 8½″. The Museum of Modern Art, Mrs. John D. Rockefeller, Jr. Purchase Fund.

KNUD MERRILD. Mirage. 1936. Gesso-wax, 19 x 21″. Lent by Dr. and Mrs. Leslie M. Maitland, West Los Angeles.

KNUD MERRILD. Man, Beast and Tree. 1934. Gesso-wax, 21 x 18″. Lent by Dr. and Mrs. Leslie M. Maitland, West Los Angeles.

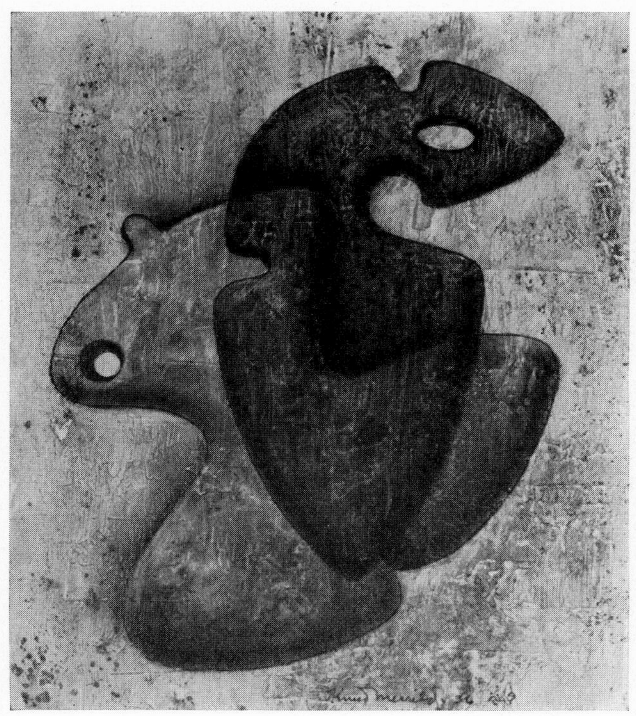

KNUD MERRILD. Archaic Form. 1936. Gesso-wax, 10½ x 8¾″. The Museum of Modern Art, Mrs. John D. Rockefeller, Jr. Purchase Fund.

MITCHELL SIPORIN

Vachel Lindsay in his poem *On the Building of Springfield* calls to the native genius:

> Record it for the grandson of your son—
> A city is not builded in a day:
> Our little town cannot complete her soul
> Till countless generations pass away.

Our poets, our writers and historians have revealed the dynamism of our cities of "broad shoulders" and the brooding loneliness of our endless prairie countryside. They have written for us of the heroic movement of our people westward and of our great leaders who over and over again insisted upon "The People, Yes."

The midwest, in the plastic arts, is only now bringing forth the artists who will reveal the physiognomy and the meaning of their place. The artist in the past has been conditioned by his life here, and yet he has always had the feeling of being lost in a world of tremendous bustle, noise and violence—this from Chicago, and from the country around an eating loneliness.

The midwestern painter and sculptor of the immediate past attached himself at first to the Greeks and to the artists of the Renaissance. Then there were the English portraitists, and in the 'nineties art in Chicago was mainly the huge Bouguereau nude swishing out of the bath off the tapestried walls of a baronial (hog, plough, or dry goods) salon on Lake Shore Drive. Caleb Bingham and Albert Ryder were thought of as indigenous and uncouth, artless (for the barons) and without pedigree.

In Walt Whitman's eagle-eye picture of our states and their meaning, a new vision found words and forms with which to reinterpret man under new conditions of life and art. Some may object to the hauling in of a writer, a poet, to prove a point in painting. Julius Meier-Graefe spoke of Rembrandt and Dostoevski in parallel, even interlocking, terms. In a similar manner can the younger generation of American artists sense kinship in the works of Whitman and José Clemente Orozco.

Of two distinct cultures and crafts, yet both Whitman and Orozco have in an epic manner revealed to us the face and meaning of their place and people. Whitman's *Leaves of Grass* and Orozco's frescoes in Guadalajara are of a piece in their deep penetration into the "souls" of peoples in two parts of our continent. From Brooklyn Bridge and from the Hospicio in Guadalajara came two voices that bridged the past, gave meaning to the present, and at once created a vision for the future and its artists. There is no synthetic regionalism here, no collecting of obvious gadgetry, no jingoistic nationalism; but instead a human democratic art, deeply thoughtful and eloquent, an art out of the lives of the people.

Through these voices we have been made aware of the scope and fullness of our environment, of the possibility of wedding modernism to a deeply moving social art. We have discovered for ourselves a richer feeling in the fabric of the history of our place. There is the big parade for us now of the past melting into the present, a parade in which each event asks epic transformation and the spirit of each historic personality asks of us nothing less than epic portrayal. We are seeking out our myth and with our growing maturity as painters we will develop towards a formal pattern for the things we say that will bind us closer to those to whom we speak.

For us there are Lincoln and Altgeld (you were wrong, Vachel Lindsay, when you said, "Sleep gently . . . eagle forgotten . . . under the stone") and the lessons of these leaders of the people will be fused into art as a permanent reminder of the heritage of our people.

For us there is the story of the reaper of Cyrus McCormick, of its influence on the life of our cities and countryside. There is the story of our constantly smoking "Pittsburgh Plus," of our industries of steel and hog, and of our agriculture of corn and wheat.

In my city today, Chicago's streets and alleys emerge from under the feathery

MITCHELL SIPORIN. The Refugees. 1939. Oil on panel, 30 x 36″. The Museum of Modern Art, Mrs. John D. Rockefeller, Jr. Purchase Fund.

brushes of the young artists of the neo-ashcan school. The abstractionists are concerned with "essentials," the dynamics of modern living. The muralists are building frescoed walls of our history. A whole new generation of Negro youth has arisen to reclaim one of the richest of all plastic heritages.

Our "little town" is in the process of completing her soul. This process can only continue in the free atmosphere of our world, our country, and our town.

MITCHELL SIPORIN

MITCHELL SIPORIN. Guerillas. 1941. Oil on canvas, 37 x 42″. Lent by the Downtown Gallery, New York.

Mitchell Siporin was born in New York City in 1910. The following year his family moved to Chicago where he has lived ever since. He studied at the Art Institute and with the painter Todros Geller.

Siporin has worked at all sorts of jobs ranging from truck driver to scene painter. In 1935 the WPA Federal Art Project gave him an opportunity to devote his time to painting, and he completed murals in the Bloom Township High School of Chicago Heights and in the Lane Technical High School in Chicago. Later, the Section of Fine Arts of the Public Buildings Administration commissioned Siporin to paint frescoes in

MITCHELL SIPORIN. Dream of a Good Life. 1941. Gouache, 23¾ x 33¾". Lent by the Downtown Gallery, New York.

the Post Office at Decatur, Illinois, in collaboration with Edward Millman and Edgar Britton.

In 1939 Siporin and Millman won the national competition to paint seventeen frescoes in the new Post Office Building in St. Louis, Missouri. They are now at work on these murals. Siporin had his first one-man show at the Downtown Gallery in New York in 1940. He is represented in the collection of the Art Institute of Chicago, the Metropolitan Museum of Art, the Museum of Modern Art and the Whitney Museum of American Art, New York, and the Smith College Museum of Art, Northampton.

MITCHELL SIPORIN. Imaginary Portrait. 1941. Gouache, 18¾ x 14½". Lent by the Downtown Gallery, New York.

EVERETT SPRUCE

Everett Spruce asked me to write his biographical sketch and furnished the notes which follow this introduction. I cannot improve upon them. His speech is telegrammatic but his work is voluble. As befits the artist, he wastes neither words nor paint. In my opinion no contemporary painter is more completely American, and few can equal the validity of his expression.

WARD LOCKWOOD. Austin, Texas, November, 1941

Born near Conway, Arkansas, 1907. Father a farmer, coming to Arkansas by wagon at the age of fourteen from the Cumberland Mountains of Tennessee. Mother born in Arkansas, the child of refugees from the carpetbag regime in Georgia.

At age of five, moved with family to farm in Ozarks. Lived there for twelve years. Country was, still is, sparsely settled. Nearest neighbor was several miles away.

At the age of seven started to school. Walked through deep woods, climbed mountains to get to the one-room building used also for Sunday school, socials, singings, square dances and political meetings.

Home was often the gathering place for singings and dances in winter months. Father was a guitarist, a little better than the usual country musician, and knew a great many of the older native folk songs and tunes, many of them originating in seventeenth

Everett Spruce. Fence Builders, West Texas. 1940. Oil on composition board, 18 x 24″. Lent by the artist.

century England and Ireland. This rich background of folk music had a strong influence on me and led to the appreciation of more profound musical forms.

Drew continually. Used any material I could find, such as school tablets and slates.

When I was very young, father took me with him to the fields, hunting, fishing, rounding up stock, looking for wild fruit, and so on. Many times I went alone over the country. Discovered the nests of birds, homes of wild animals, strange trees, dramatic storms, swollen streams. So, very early, felt an intimacy with nature that has influenced whatever I have said or wanted to say in painting.

Went to high school at Mulberry, Arkansas. Made the most of the opportunity of using the school's fine library. While in school raised crops of corn and cotton.

By this time I had one sister and four brothers. Father had too heavy a load to be able to contribute to my education, and I saw I would have a hard time getting an education in art. Decided long before this that I must somehow become an artist.

EVERETT SPRUCE. Mending Rock Fence. 1937. Oil on masonite, 20 x 24". Lent by Southern Methodist University, Dallas, Texas.

Up to this time I had never seen a real artist or a good painting. One day I was visiting the farm of my aunt when Olin Travis and his wife Kathryn Hail came to inquire if they could paint a certain view of the farm. This was one of the most exciting days in my life. Travis had opened an art school in Dallas, Texas that year. He offered me a scholarship for the following year.

I cleared about twenty-five dollars on my crop after debts had been paid, and set out for Dallas. Was given a three year janitor job in the school and studied there from 1926 to 1929. Contacts there with students and artists were wonderful although I nearly starved.

Travis was very sympathetic. Impressed on me the importance of being a real artist. He introduced us to the work of modern artists, making us understand them. He owned

Everett Spruce. The Hawk. 1939. Oil on composition board, 19⅜ x 23½″. The Museum of Modern Art, Mrs. John D. Rockefeller, Jr. Purchase Fund.

a fine collection of recorded music, and I was profoundly impressed by listening to it and hearing him talk about it. Contact with this man's ideas and generous personality has had more to do with my becoming an artist than any other thing.

While in art school I met Alice Kramer, a student, and we were married in 1935.

The last year in art school Thomas M. Stell came to teach life drawing—from him I received invaluable instruction and a much clearer idea of the old masters.

In 1930 I started to work in the Dallas Museum of Fine Arts as general workman—packing, shipping and installing exhibitions. Later did research, conducted gallery tours and taught museum classes. In 1935 was made registrar and assistant to the director. All this experience broadened my outlook, made me humble toward art. With the exception of three summers, my painting was limited to nights and one day

Everett Spruce. The Watering Trough. 1941. Oil on canvas, 18 x 24¼″. Lent by the artist.

a week during these ten years with the museum. Continually submitted work to national exhibitions. Was lucky in a few instances. This was a great encouragement.

In 1937 twin daughters and in 1939 a son were born to us.

In 1940 Ward Lockwood telephoned to offer me a position on the staff of the newly formed Department of Art in the College of Fine Arts of the University of Texas in Austin. I accepted. Having half of my time to spend at my own work, it is my first real opportunity to concentrate on the business of being a painter.

Everett Spruce

Everett Spruce has had two one-man shows in New York—at the Delphic Studios in 1937 and at the Hudson D. Walker Gallery in 1938. He is represented in the collections of the Dallas Museum of Fine Arts and the Museum of Modern Art, New York.

CATALOG OF THE EXHIBITION

All works are lent by the artists unless otherwise credited. A star preceding the title indicates that the work is illustrated.

DARREL AUSTIN

* Europa and the Bull. October 1940. Oil on canvas, 30 x 36″. Lent by the Detroit Institute of Arts.

Eclipse of the Moon. October 1940. Oil on canvas, 18 x 20″. Lent by the Perls Galleries, New York.

* Catamount. November 1940. Oil on canvas, 20 x 24″. The Museum of Modern Art, Mrs. John D. Rockefeller, Jr. Purchase Fund.

The Tree. January 1941. Oil on canvas, 20 x 24″. Lent by Edwin J. Lukas, White Plains, N. Y.

The Tiger. February 1941. Oil on canvas, 30 x 36″. Lent by the Perls Galleries, New York.

* The Legend. March 1941. Oil on canvas, 30 x 24″. Lent by the Perls Galleries, New York.

* The Black Beast. April 1941. Oil on canvas, 24 x 30″. Lent by the Smith College Museum of Art, Northampton, Mass.

* The Vixen. April 1941. Oil on canvas, 24 x 20″. Lent by the Museum of Fine Arts, Boston.

The Tree Legend. May 1941. Oil on canvas, 30 x 36″. Lent by the Perls Galleries, New York.

Performance. July 1941. Oil on canvas, 39 x 48″. Lent by the Perls Galleries, New York.

* Girl in the Brook. August 1941. Oil on canvas, 20 x 15″. Lent by Miss Helen Resor, Greenwich, Conn.

Beast Enchanted. August 1941. Oil on canvas, 20 x 24″. Lent by Stanley Rogers Resor, Greenwich, Conn.

The Primate. August 1941. Oil on canvas, 20 x 15″. Lent by Mr. and Mrs. Lee A. Ault, New Canaan, Conn.

5 drawings. Summer 1939. Pencil and crayon on wet paper, 14¼ x 11″ and 23 x 14½″. Lent by the Perls Galleries, New York.

HYMAN BLOOM

* Skeleton. *c.* 1936. Oil on canvas, 12 x 68″. Lent by Nat Sharfman, Boston.

The Fish. *c.* 1936. Oil on canvas, 16 x 40⅛″.

Circus Rider. *c.* 1937. Oil on plywood, 20 x 23¼″. Lent by Miss Margaret Prall, Berkeley, Cal.

The Baby. *c.* 1938. Oil on canvas, 16 x 31″. Lent by George Palmer, Boston.

The Stove. 1938. Oil on canvas, 48 x 38⅜″. Lent by the Massachusetts WPA Art Program.

* The Christmas Tree. *c.* 1939. Oil on canvas, 54 x 35″.

The Christmas Tree. 1939. Oil on canvas, 50 x 28″. Lent by the Massachusetts WPA Art Program.

The Christmas Tree. 1939. Oil on canvas, 52 x 31″. Lent by the Massachusetts WPA Art Program.

* The Chandelier. *c.* 1940. Oil on canvas, 72 x 36″.

* The Synagogue. *c.* 1940. Oil on canvas, 65¼ x 46¼″.

* The Synagogue. *c.* 1940. Oil on canvas, 39 x 30⅛″. Lent by the Massachusetts WPA Art Program.

* Jew with the Torah. *c.* 1940. Oil on canvas, 33 x 35″.

The Bride. 1941. Oil on canvas, 20 x 48″.

RAYMOND BREININ

* White House. 1938. Oil on canvas, 30 x 40⅛″. Lent by the WPA Art Program, Washington, D. C.

The Edge of the City. 1939. Gouache, 16 x 27¼″. Lent by the Fogg Museum of Art, Harvard University, Cambridge.

* One Morning. 1939. Gouache, 16⅝ x 27⅝″. The Museum of Modern Art, Mrs. John D. Rockefeller, Jr. Purchase Fund.

* Interior with Ancestor. 1939. Gouache, 16½ x 28″. Lent by the Downtown Gallery, New York.

The Beach. 1940. Gouache, 19 x 28″. Lent by the Downtown Gallery, New York.

Ancient Warriors. 1941. Oil on canvas, 32 x 40″. Lent by the Downtown Gallery, New York.

Along the Beach. 1941. Oil on composition board, 24 x 40″. Lent by the Downtown Gallery, New York.

* The Lover's Return. 1941. Oil on canvas, 30 x 40″. Lent by the Downtown Gallery, New York.
* At Golgotha. 1941. Oil on composition board, 30 x 48″. Lent by the Downtown Gallery, New York.
* The Night. 1941. Gouache, 22 x 30″. Lent by the Downtown Gallery, New York.

The Saint of the Flaming City. 1941. Oil on canvas, 30 x 40″. Lent by the Downtown Gallery, New York.

SAMUEL CASHWAN

* Torso. 1936. Limestone, 23¾″ high. Lent by the WPA Art Program, Washington, D. C.
* Torso. 1937. Limestone, 22″ high.

Fountain Group. 1937. Green marble, 14″ high.

* Bather. 1937. Green marble, 14″ high.
* The Prophet. 1937. Terra cotta, 9½″ high.
* Baptism. 1938. Terra cotta, 7⅛″ high.
* Kneeling Torso. 1938. Terra cotta, 12″ high.
* Rising Figure. 1939. Mankato stone, 19½″ high. Lent by the Michigan WPA Art Program.

Suzanna. 1939. Terra cotta, 9⅞″ high.

Jacob and the Angel. 1939. Terra cotta, 14″ high.

* Seated Figure. 1939. Terra cotta, 7½″ high.

Standing figure. 1939. Terra cotta, 14″ high.

Nude with Drapery. 1940. Terra cotta, 8¾″ high. Lent by Charles Pollock, Detroit.

* Shelter. 1940. Terra cotta, 9″ high.

FRANCIS CHAPIN

Tourists in Taxco. 1933. Watercolor, 10¼ x 14½″.

Child with Red Scarf. 1936. Oil on canvas, 16 x 14″.

The Ferry Store. 1938. Oil on masonite, 16 x 24″.

* Spring Sunlight. 1938. Oil on canvas, 29 x 36″.

Outing. 1938. Watercolor, 8¾ x 11¾″.

* Children at Breakfast. 1939. Oil on canvas, 28 x 40″.

Blithe Summer. 1939. Watercolor, 13 x 9½″.

Vermont Landscape. 1939. Watercolor, 12¾ x 19½″.

Deep Snow in Chicago. 1940. Oil on canvas, 30 x 25″.

October. 1940. Watercolor, 14 x 20″.

Flowers on Camp Stool. 1940. Watercolor, 18 x 12″.

* Rutland Station. 1940. Watercolor, 21½ x 14¾″.

On the Kalamazoo. 1941. Oil on canvas, 36 x 29″.

Girl Rowing. 1941. Watercolor, 19½ x 13½″.

* Nude. 1941. Watercolor, 17½ x 12″.

EMMA LU DAVIS

* Grotesque Bull. 1934. Terra cotta, 15¼″ long. Lent by the Boyer Galleries, New York. (Illustrated opposite.)
* Bantam Rooster. 1934. Painted wood with copper, 13¾″ high. Lent by the Whitney Museum of American Art, New York.
* Cosmic Presence. 1934. Wood, 66″ long.
* Black Bull. 1935. Wood, 34½″ high, 51″ long. Lent by Mrs. Walter Davenport, Winsted, Conn.
* Hsiao Di-Di. 1936. Walnut, 6¾″ high.
* Head of Chinese Red Army Soldier. 1936. Walnut, 9¾″ high. Lent by Mrs. Jan de Graaff, Portland, Ore.

Cat Running. 1938. Wood, 23″ long. Lent by Mrs. Jan de Graaff, Portland, Ore.

Dancers: over-mantel relief for Student Union Building. 1939. Walnut, polychrome, 48 x 48″. Lent by Reed College, Portland, Ore.

Colt (Memorial to Henry). 1939. Glazed terra cotta, 21⅛″ long. Lent by Edward B. Rowan, Falls Church, Va.

Bull. 1940. Glazed terra cotta, 15″ long. Lent by Mrs. Henry L. Corbett, Portland, Ore.

* "Handies." 1939–41. Wood.
* "Folded" Cat. 1941. Terra cotta, 16″ long. Lent by the Oregon Ceramic Studio, Portland.

"Folded" Cat. 1941. Terra cotta, 13¼″ long. Lent by Dr. A. Gurney Kimberley, Portland, Ore.

MORRIS GRAVES

Eagle of the Inner Eye. Gouache, 20¾ x 20¾″.

Owl of the Inner Eye. Gouache, 20¾ x 36⅝″.

Unnamed Bird of the Inner Eye. Gouache, 22 x 39″.

Dove of the Inner Eye. Gouache, 20⅝ x 36¾″.

* Little Known Bird of the Inner Eye. Gouache, 21 x 36¾″.
* Bird Singing in the Moonlight. Gouache, 26¾ x 30⅛″.
* Bird in the Moonlight. Gouache, 25 x 30¼″. Lent by Mr. and Mrs. Charles Ross, Seattle.
* Shore Birds. Gouache, 25⅞ x 28⅞″. Lent by Lee Foley, Seattle.

EMMA LU DAVIS. Grotesque Bull. 1934. Terra cotta, 15¼" long. Lent by the Boyer Galleries, New York.

Veiled Bird. Gouache, 19¾ x 33¾". Lent by Mr. and Mrs. Hollis Farwell, Seattle.

In the Night. Gouache, 27 x 29⅞".

Chalice. Gouache, 30⅝ x 26".

* Snake and Moon. Watercolor and gouache, 25½ x 30¼".

* Blind Bird. Gouache, 30⅛ x 27".

Woodpeckers. Gouache, 30½ x 26". Lent by Dr. Richard E. Fuller, Seattle.

* Constant Journey. Gouache, 12⅝ x 16⅛".

* Purification. Series of nine gouaches, each 12½ x 16⅛".

Destruction of Rome. Two gouaches, each 12½ x 16⅛".

Roman, English, *French and German Nightfall Pieces. Series in pencil and red ink, each 26 x 21".

* Message no. 6. One of a series, tempera and wax, 12 x 16½". Lent by the WPA Art Program, Washington, D. C.

JOSEPH HIRSCH

* Masseur Tom. 1933. Oil on canvas, 80 x 47¼". Lent by Associated American Artists, New York.

The Champion. 1933. Pastel monochrome, 24¼ x 11⅝". Lent by Arthur Judson, New York.

Shanghai Beggar Woman. 1936. Pencil, 18¼ x 12½". Lent by Herman Shulman, New York.

* Two Men. 1937. Oil on canvas, 18⅛ x 48¼". The Museum of Modern Art, Mrs. John D. Rockefeller, Jr. Purchase Fund.

* Landscape with Tear Gas. 1937. Oil on canvas, 23 x 31". Lent by Associated American Artists, New York.

Gabriel. 1937. Oil on panel, 8 x 12". Lent by Miss Aline MacMahon, New York.

Clown. 1938. Watercolor, 20 x 28½". Lent by the WPA Art Program, Washington, D. C.

Portrait of an Old Man. 1939. Oil on canvas, 44 x 30". Lent by Associated American Artists, New York.

* The Warrior. 1940. Oil on canvas, 32 x 18". Lent by Associated American Artists, New York.

* Vermont Roof. 1940. Oil on canvas, 10¼ x 24½". Lent by Associated American Artists, New York.

New Year's Still Life. 1941. Oil on canvas, 12 x 18¼". Lent by Mrs. Marquis James, Pleasantville, N. Y.

Clowns and the News. 1941. Oil on canvas, 23 x 42 1/8". Lent by Jesse Lilienthal, Hillsborough, Cal.

* The Confidence. 1941. Oil on canvas, 14 x 18". Lent by Samuel Spewack, New Hope, Pa.

* The Drink. 1941. Oil on canvas, 13 x 23". Lent by Mr. and Mrs. Benjamin Laskin, Germantown, Pa.

Chinese Father and Son. 1941. Charcoal, 18 x 11". Lent by Associated American Artists, New York.

Lunch Counter. 1941. Oil on canvas, 15 1/4 x 37 1/2". Lent by Herman Shulman, New York.

* Chinese-American. 1941. Oil on panel, 10 x 8". Lent by Associated American Artists, New York.

DONAL HORD

* The Aztec. 1936–37. Diorite, 52" high. Lent by the San Diego State College, through the Southern California WPA Art Program, Los Angeles.

La Cubana. 1937–38. Obsidian, 11 3/4" high. Lent by the Dalzell Hatfield Galleries, Los Angeles.

* Mexican Mother and Child. 1938. Tennessee marble, 16 3/4" high. Lent by the Franklin D. Roosevelt Library, Hyde Park, through the WPA Art Program, Washington, D. C.

* Mexican Beggar. 1938. Columbia marble, 12 3/4" high. Lent by the WPA Art Program, Washington, D. C.

* Veiled Figure. 1938. Tennessee marble, 15 1/4" high. Lent by the WPA Art Program, Washington, D. C.

CHARLES HOWARD

Souvenir. 1935. Gouache, 13 1/2 x 20 3/4". Lent by Mrs. Morris Cafritz, Washington, D. C.

Cave. 1937. Gouache, 9 7/8 x 12 7/8".

Omen. 1938. Gouache, 9 1/4 x 14 3/8".

Collection. 1938. Gouache, 14 x 21".

Rumor. 1938. Gouache, 21 1/4 x 29 1/4".

* The Cage. 1938. Gouache, 21 1/8 x 29 1/8".

Precinct. 1938. Gouache, 17 3/4 x 26 1/2". Lent by Dr. and Mrs. Lindel French, San Francisco.

Presage I. 1938. Gouache, 14 3/8 x 21 3/8".

The Inmate. 1939. Oil on canvas, 11 3/4 x 15 5/8".

Hare-Corner. 1939. Gouache, 26 3/8 x 35 1/2". Lent by Mrs. John Galen Howard, Berkeley, Cal.

* Generation. 1940. Oil on canvas, 15 1/8 x 18".

Motivization. 1940. Oil on canvas, 19 3/4 x 23 7/8".

Reflection. 1941. Oil on canvas, 24 1/8 x 34 1/8".

* Trinity. 1941. Oil on canvas, 24 1/8 x 34 1/4".

Presentiment. 1941. Oil on canvas, 14 x 18 1/8".

RICO LEBRUN

Woman Looking Up. 1936. Ink and chalk, 25 x 19". Lent by Mr. and Mrs. Max Schott, New York.

Running Woman. 1936. Ink and chalk, 25 x 19". Lent by the Hon. and Mrs. Robert Woods Bliss, Santa Barbara.

Thus He Died. 1939. Ink and chalk, 19 x 25". Lent by Mr. and Mrs. Hugh Chisholm, Beverly Hills, Cal.

* Bather. 1940. Oil on canvas, 50 x 30".

Musician. 1940. Ink, 25 1/8 x 18 7/8".

Harmonium Player. 1940. Ink, 25 x 19". Lent by Mr. and Mrs. Donald J. Bear, Santa Barbara.

Portrait of a Man. 1940. Ink and chalk, 40 x 30". Lent by Wright Ludington, Santa Barbara.

Slaughter House. 1940. Oil on canvas, 20 x 34".

* Migration to Nowhere. 1941. Gouache on board, 30 x 48".

San Gennaro's Mob. 1941. Gouache on board, 24 x 48".

Sirocco. 1941. Oil on wood, 15 x 20".

* A Penny. 1941. Oil and tempera on board, 19 x 24".

Birds in the Sky. 1941. Ink and chalk, 25 x 19". Lent by Mr. and Mrs. Arthur Sachs, Santa Barbara.

Crucifixion. 1941. Pencil, 17 1/4 x 9 1/2". Lent by Mr. and Mrs. Channing Peake, Santa Barbara.

Woman. 1941. Ink and chalk, 40 x 30". Lent by Mr. and Mrs. Joseph T. Ryerson, Chicago.

* Ortensia. 1941. Ink and chalk on board, 40 x 30". Lent by George P. Raymond, New York.

Ortensia Seated. 1941. Pencil, 25 x 19".

* Seated Clown. 1941. Ink and chalk on board, 40 x 30". Lent by the Santa Barbara Museum of Art.

* The Relatives of San Gennaro. 1941. Ink, 6 1/2 x 8 1/4".

* The Ragged One. 1941. Ink and chalk, 25 x 19".

JACK LEVINE

* The Feast of Pure Reason. 1937. Oil on canvas, 42 x 48". Lent by the WPA Art Program, Washington, D. C.

String Quartette. 1937. Oil on composition board, 48 x 67". Lent by the Downtown Gallery, New York.

* The Street. 1938. Oil tempera and oil on canvas, 60 x 84". Lent by the WPA Art Program, Washington, D. C.

* The Millionaire. 1938. Oil on canvas, 34 x 16". Lent by David L. Podell, New York.

The Syndicate. 1939. Oil on canvas, 30 x 45". Lent by the Downtown Gallery, New York.

Neighborhood Physician. 1939. Oil on canvas, 48 x 30". Lent by the Downtown Gallery, New York.

King David Playing His Harp. 1940. Tempera on wood, 10 x 8". Lent by Mrs. James S. Plaut, Cambridge, Mass.

King Solomon. 1941. Oil on wood, 12 x 9". Lent by the Downtown Gallery, New York.

* Planning Solomon's Temple. 1941. Oil on composition board, 10 x 8". Lent by Herman Shulman, New York.

* Card Game. 1941. Oil on canvas, 16 x 14". Lent by Mr. and Mrs. Samuel A. Lewisohn, New York.

* The Banquet. 1941. Oil on canvas, 25¼ x 30". Lent by the Downtown Gallery, New York.

HELEN LUNDEBERG

* Artist, Flower and Hemispheres. 1934. Oil on celotex, 23¾" x 30". Lent by the San Francisco Museum of Art.

Plant and Animal Analogies. 1935. Oil on celotex, 24 x 30".

Relative Magnitude. 1936. Oil on masonite, 30 x 26⅛".

Microcosm and Macrocosm. 1937. Oil on masonite, 28⅛ x 13½".

* Eyes. 1938-39. Oil on masonite, 16 x 13¼".

* The Tree. 1938. Oil on masonite, 30½ x 24".

FLETCHER MARTIN

* Trouble in Frisco. 1938. Oil on canvas, 30 x 36". The Museum of Modern Art, Mrs. John D. Rockefeller, Jr. Purchase Fund.

Exit in Color. 1939. Oil on canvas, 40 x 30". Lent by the Midtown Galleries, New York.

* Temptation in Tonopah. 1940. Oil on wood, 18 x 12". Lent by Mrs. Stanley Resor, Greenwich, Conn.

* Out at Home. 1940. Oil on canvas, 23 x 44". Lent by the Midtown Galleries, New York.

* Stormy Weather. 1941. Oil on canvas, 40 x 24". Lent by the Midtown Galleries, New York.

Self Portrait. 1941. Oil on canvas, 19 x 24". Lent by the Midtown Galleries, New York.

OCTAVIO MEDELLIN

* Primitive Woman. 1935. White limestone, 25¼" high.

Mad Moses. 1936. Gray sandstone, 21¼" high.

* At the Stake. 1938. Wood, 21" high.

Doe and Fawn. 1939. Rose sandstone, 19" high.

* Penitentes. 1940. Cast stone, 21¾" high.

* Waiting Figure. 1940. Red sandstone, 23" high. Lent by Mr. and Mrs. Frank Rosengren, San Antonio, Texas.

* Holy Roller. 1941. Red terra cotta, 22" high. Lent by Vladimir Golschmann, St. Louis.

KNUD MERRILD

Anthropometric. 1930. Oil on panel, 14 x 12".

* Man, Beast and Tree. 1934. Gesso-wax, 21 x 18". Lent by Dr. and Mrs. Leslie M. Maitland, West Los Angeles.

Self Portrait. 1934. Gesso-wax, 24 x 20".

* Herma. 1935. Gesso-wax, 10½ x 8½". The Museum of Modern Art, Mrs. John D. Rockefeller, Jr. Purchase Fund.

Fata Morgana. 1935. Oil on canvas, 20 x 15".

Knowledge and Life. 1935. Gesso-wax, 32 x 24".

Siamese Twins. 1935. Gesso-wax, 20 x 15".

Hermaphrodite. 1935. Gesso-wax, 11 x 8½". Lent by the Weyhe Gallery, New York.

To Bumse. 1935. Gesso-wax, 21 x 18". Lent by Dr. and Mrs. Leslie M. Maitland, West Los Angeles.

Third Month. 1935. Oil on masonite, 18 x 12¼". Lent by the Los Angeles County Museum.

* Synthesis. *c.* 1936. Gesso-wax, 10 x 9¼". The Museum of Modern Art, Mrs. John D. Rockefeller, Jr. Purchase Fund.

* Archaic Form. 1936. Gesso-wax, 10½ x 8¾". The Museum of Modern Art, Mrs. John D. Rockefeller, Jr. Purchase Fund.

Abstraction. 1936. Gesso-wax, 20 x 15".

* Mirage. 1936. Gesso-wax, 19 x 21". Lent by Dr. and Mrs. Leslie M. Maitland, West Los Angeles.

MITCHELL SIPORIN

* The Refugees. 1939. Oil on panel, 30 x 36″. The Museum of Modern Art, Mrs. John D. Rockefeller, Jr. Purchase Fund.

Homecoming After Flight. 1940. Gouache, 21 x 31″. Lent by the Art Institute of Chicago.

* Guerillas. 1941. Oil on canvas, 37 x 42″. Lent by the Downtown Gallery, New York.

Respite. 1941. Oil on canvas, 35 x 50″. Lent by the Downtown Gallery, New York.

* Dream of a Good Life. 1941. Gouache, 23¾ x 33¾″. Lent by the Downtown Gallery, New York.

* Imaginary Portrait. 1941. Gouache, 18¾ x 14½″. Lent by the Downtown Gallery, New York.

Four Girls. 1941. Gouache, 28 x 17¾″. Lent by the Downtown Gallery, New York.

In the Red Lantern. 1941. Gouache, 25 x 18¾″. Lent by the Downtown Gallery, New York.

EVERETT SPRUCE

Autumn, Southwest Texas. 1936. Oil on composition board, 24 x 30″. Lent by Mrs. H. L. Edwards, Dallas, Texas.

* Mending Rock Fence. 1937. Oil on masonite, 20 x 24″. Lent by Southern Methodist University, Dallas, Texas.

The Twins. 1939-40. Oil on canvas, 19⅛ x 23¼″. Lent by the Dallas Museum of Fine Arts, Dallas, Texas.

* The Hawk. 1939. Oil on composition board, 19⅜ x 23½″. The Museum of Modern Art, Mrs. John D. Rockefeller, Jr. Purchase Fund.

Night in West Texas. 1940. Oil on composition board, 18 x 24″.

* Fence Builders, West Texas. 1940. Oil on composition board, 18 x 24″.

The Hollow Tree. 1940. Oil on composition board, 15 x 19″.

* The Watering Trough. 1941. Oil on canvas, 18 x 24¼″.

In the Davis Mountains. 1941. Oil on canvas, 16⅛ x 24″.

West of Austin. 1941. Oil on composition board, 18 x 24″.

The Night Watchman. 1941. Oil on canvas, 25 x 28¼″.

River at Night. 1941. Oil on canvas, 28 x 34¼″.

Fisherman. 1941. Oil on composition board, 20 x 24″.

The Fox. 1941. Oil on composition board, 20 x 24″.

Morning. 1941. Oil on composition board, 21 x 24″.

SIX THOUSAND FIVE HUNDRED COPIES OF THIS BOOK HAVE BEEN PRINTED IN JANUARY, 1942, FOR THE TRUSTEES OF THE MUSEUM OF MODERN ART BY THE AMERICAN BOOK–STRATFORD PRESS, NEW YORK.